Windham's Rembrandt

The True Story of the First Prison Art Teacher in Texas

JAMES L. HUMPHRIES & JONATHAN R. HUMPHRIES

Windham's Rembrandt: The True Story of a Prison Art Teacher
Copyright © 2012 by Jonathan Humphries/Humphries Creative Works

ALL RIGHTS RESERVED

For information about this title or to order other books and/or electronic media, contact the publisher:
Humphries Creative Works
www.jonathanhumphries.com

978-0-9859040-0-5 – Black and White Print Book
978-0-9859040-1-2 – Color Print Book
978-0-9859040-2-9 – eBooks

Printed in the United States of America

Cover concept by Henner Zeller and Jonathan Humphries
Book jacket layout and Interior design by 1106design.com

TABLE OF CONTENTS

"The need of individuals to communicate with others through artistic expression is not diminished by the experience of incarceration."

—W. J. Estelle Jr., Director,
Texas Department of Corrections, 1978

PREFACE

THIS IS NOT SIMPLY ANOTHER STORY of prison life, because James L. Humphries was never an inmate, or even a guard or warden. This is the story of how pioneering an art program for incarcerated felons changed his life and put him in the unique position to see a very different side of some otherwise dangerous men. Many years ago James left those prisons, but the memories still remain as clear as if he were there only days ago.

What James, or Jim as he liked to be called, learned from those men in uniform, whether they wore trustee white or TDC (Texas Department of Criminal Justice) gray, has proven invaluable to his life as a father, teacher and artist. But these stories are not only about him. Each story will also paint a picture of life inside a state penitentiary through the eyes of not only inmates and guards, but also of the non-security staff, who rarely get the chance to tell their tale. Those people are the teachers, nurses and administrators of corrections. Jim has preserved their memories and those of his own as a series of short stories, so maybe you too can learn from them. Herein are Jim's impressions of the inmates and troubled patients who were locked in their houses, meaning their cells, and of those who walked freely among them.

The artist in Jim was taken aback by the mentality of his students. The inmates he encountered had a hidden angst inside them, as if each one kept a sort of beast within. This beast is how Jim characterized the alter ego that causes irrational, sociopathic behavior. The beast howled in the minds of Jim's inmate students, as it slowly tore their souls asunder. The inmates tried to stifle this howling with their prison jobs and pastimes, but no matter how hard they tried, many could never quell its anger.

Jim's job seemed simple enough and that was to teach these inmates how to express themselves visually. Yet in doing so, this task called upon him to search their collective psyche and salvage any part of their souls that still remained intact. Jim's work has always been a spiritual endeavor, as well as a aesthetic one, but after taking this job, Jim found that he could inspire his students and help bolster their self-worth, in spite of whatever crime they had committed. Their crimes had already been judged and their punishment prescribed. And in my opinion as Jim's son, there is no adequate way to measure the strain a man endures from incarceration. Society can physically imprison a man's body, but only the man himself can incarcerate his own spirit.

Many of the men Jim taught had long embraced a convoluted perspective of the world. They spoke highly of their crimes, rarely finding any fault in what horrible things they had done. Since their actions were in accordance to their own understanding of ethics, any recognition of guilt on their part was close to impossible. They talked about a "code of the street," not the law of the land. It was Jim's conception that prisons are full of men who live in contradiction to everything society seeks to preserve by the tenets of law.

However, among the scores of morally deficient convicts, Jim did meet many good men during those twelve years. Some of them had led simple, honest lives, free from ill fortune and malice. They had families, went to church, and coached little leagues. But all it takes is just a fraction of a second for the beast to transform good men into agents of deceit, terror, or even death. Jim could see how they too were victims, only that their crimes were against themselves.

It is this beast that you will read about, for it represents an integral part of human behavior. It is the Omega to our Alpha, our constant shadow self. If you allow it to control your life, it will destroy you and everything you love. The threads of reason weaving your conscious mind into the moral fabric of society will unravel, and between those moments of confusion and extreme emotions, the beast will present seemingly attractive alternatives to acceptable yet lawful behavior. It is in those fleeting moments that very good people can do the most horrible things.

— Jonathan R. Humphries

Those who work and study in a correctional education program must be constantly aware the beast prowls the edge of reason, between the limit of light and the beginning of darkness.

PROPOSAL

IT ALL BEGAN ON a midsummer's day in 1972, a year when Houston lent an especially generous dose of humidity to the already sweltering Southern sun. No matter how hard the diner's air conditioning labored furiously above me, it didn't affect the ambient temperature much. It mostly just rattled and dripped water on unsuspecting diners as they walked through the entrance. There is just no beating down such heat. It seeps into every room and smothers whatever kind air still lingers. But none of this was new to a Houstonian like me. You learn to improvise, adapt and overcome. Oh, and order every drink with extra ice!

Sitting across from me was Dr. Lane Murray, a Windham School District representative. Windham is special because all of the students are inmates housed by the Texas Department of Corrections, and all classes were held inside prison walls. Dr. Murray had telephoned me to discuss the first state-accredited art program for male inmates. The pilot program was set to begin in a place I had never heard of, a prison north of Houston, near the small town of Huntsville, called the Ferguson Unit.

"So, why me?" I asked.

"You come highly recommended, Mr. Humphries," she stated. "The chairman of the art department at Sam Houston State informed me you might be a good candidate for the proposed position. I also hear you're a former Marine, that you're certified to teach art, and since you are sitting here with me, you might be looking for a new line of work." She paused to study me as if to gauge my worth, then continued. "I'll surmise you can guess the working conditions at TDC."

A job offer to teach art in a prison was completely unexpected. I had commanded Marine units for years, but this was a whole new ball game. Yet, felons are in some ways similar to soldiers. They both live by a code of honor, loyalty and respect. The major difference is that while Marines fight for God and country, felons fight for money and power. Another difference is when a young man enters boot camp, he is quickly broken down, then built up into a soldier ready to live and die for his country. A criminal's life breaks him down but fails to properly build him into a mature, accountable man. Almost inevitably, he is caged up with other overgrown boys who fight over childish things, like what TV channel to watch or whose turn it is on the basketball court. As time goes on, incarceration further breaks down a man, beats him to a pulp, and leaves him to fend for himself. Friends and families turn their backs, leaving the man to live alone in a lifeless cage.

Many questions ran through my head during those weeks leading up to my decision. Will my classes be taken seriously? How can they be of any use to a felon? Will I be able to step in and help these men understand that they have something more to offer the world than a life of crime? The answers were unclear to me but one practical thing was: I was between jobs and the steady paycheck would be nice.

Besides, as Dr. Murray was making it clear in as few words as possible, I was the one for the job. She was a woman who commanded respect and expected loyalty, a quality that reminded me of a female Marine colonel I had once admired. Both women possessed a benevolence that was tempered by a no-nonsense "don't-make-me-tell-you-again" kind of attitude.

"Yes, I'm aware of the risks," I replied. "Working with inmates is new to me, but I've never backed down from a challenge. I've thought about it, and realized I may be able to do some good for those men."

"Well, Mr. Humphries, your positive attitude is exactly what our inmates need. Life is tough enough for them, so we've got to do as much as we can as educators to make their lives better. It's because we're not security personnel that we're able to view inmates in a different light. Our perspective can give the inmates a different sense of worth when they're in our classes. You'll have to construct an appropriate art program that does this and hopefully more. Just don't fudge this up, because I have a lot riding on this."

"I won't let you down, ma'am," I promised.

"Good," she said with a smile and a sigh of relief. "Next, I'd like for you to come to Huntsville and visit the Ferguson Unit. It's a place for first-time offenders but don't let their youth fool you. While some are just scared schoolboys, others are already hardened criminals. You'll run the gamut at Ferguson but I think you can handle it."

"I'll do my best, ma'am."

"Mr. Humphries, it's been a pleasure but I have a long drive back to Huntsville." She took a card from her wallet and scribbled an address on the rear. "Take this and use it if anyone gives you any problems." She stood up and to leave, then added, "Welcome to Windham."

Her card read, "Dr. Lane Murray, Superintendent, Windham School District," and on the back, there was a handwritten address for Ferguson Unit. That was my step into the world of the incarcerated, into a concrete and steel labyrinth where another world thrives and the beast roams free. Nothing could prepare me for what the next decade would bring.

First Days at the Ferguson Unit

Red Birds

Flip-flap, glide, stall.
Flip-flap, glide, stall.

THE RADIO IN MY 1962 TRAVELALL hadn't worked for months. I couldn't afford a new one, so I settled on a flock of cardinals to provide the soundtrack for the journey down Farm Road to Market Road (FM) 247, a road that's always full of surprises. Creeks, swollen from the rain, would regularly flood parts of the road, sending fish swimming over the bridges rather than under them. Cattle drives would force all traffic to a standstill during the summer months. And for reasons beyond my understanding, the local population had a penchant for driving on the left side of the road.

I still remember how those red birds flew lazily through the Texas sun. For miles we enjoyed the landscape together in a harmonious sonata. They sang a melody of tweets and chirps, and my Travelall rumbled out the hypnotic rhythm of the highway tarmac. Life was grand for miles, until my avian friends started to close in on me. There was plenty of space to fly across the road, though the birds seemed to prefer the route directly in front of my Travelall. At least some were smart enough to fly over me but an unlucky few wound up plastered to the truck's grille: "Just the wrong place at the wrong time." That was an explanation I'd regularly hear from inmates who told me their stories about why or how they fell, or what bad timing brought them to prison.

Mile upon mile of Texas landscape passed in a blur of dry grass, crude fence posts and rusted wire. Then, in the middle of nowhere, everything changed. Creosote wood replaced the rustic planks. Fresh barbed wire hung taut between the tar-covered posts. In the distance, white-uniformed inmates rhythmically hoed the earth under

the watchful eyes of men on horseback, who, I would later learn, were called the "High Riders." The Texas prison system is divided up into separate entities known as Units. I had arrived at the Ferguson Unit.

A healthy expanse of pastures and farmland surrounded a two-story, red-bricked building. The aroma of the prison farm scented the morning air, and depending on whether the wind was blowing from the barn or the fields, the air could have the smell of freshly tilled earth or the rank stench of animal manure. Luck for me I arrived on a still day.

I pulled into the parking lot, made sure to lock my truck, and strolled over to the front gate, where the Radio Picket guard was stationed. From his twenty-foot tower, the uniformed guard lowered a tin pail to retrieve my identification. It felt a bit medieval, having my essentials hoisted up into a tower by a bucket on a string. Then again, nothing from this point on would be close to familiar. For a couple of minutes, the guard peered down at me from his turret while he studied my identification, matching the man at his gate with the one in the ID photo. More minutes passed before the bucket lowered, and then, the gates into the prison grounds lurched open.

Buzz, chunk. Buzz, chunk—The unmistakable sound of mechanized prison gates.

White-uniformed trustees were mowing the grass with push reels, cleaning the flowerbeds and watering the marigolds that had been carefully planted along the sidewalks. Our Old Glory waved proudly above the Lone Star, almost lending me a feeling of being back on a Marine base. Inside the front entrance stood a small, wood-paneled lobby with display cases for inmate craftwork. Prison-made vinyl couches with wooded armrests were placed abreast various plants from the prison greenhouse. It seemed like most everything was made, planted or designed by the inmates.

This final door to the main passage hall was held by a massive, sliding metal bar that could only be moved manually by another guard located in a green, barred enclosure known as the Control Picket. From here, the guard in the Control Picket checked purses, lunch bags, and any other container an employee wanted to bring inside.

"Nothing can be brought inside that'll harm an inmate," barked the guard. "What may be a common thing to you can kill a man in here, got that? You're new here, so you had better not forget it." Once an employee passed beyond the Control Picket, he or she had to be on constant alert. I'd read in my briefing papers that prison employees like me were rated as a "zero value" to inmates in a hostage situation. Not the most reassuring thing to read before you start a new job.

Inside Ferguson, inmate privacy was at a minimum. During my orientation tour, I noticed how the showers were open and the lavatory stalls were barely waist high. But the inside temperature was surprisingly cool, given the heat outside. I walked by a couple of inmates mopping the floor, close enough for them to notice though neither showed any interest in my presence.

Passing another man without acknowledgment was a bit unsettling, but it would be a treatment I needed to get used to. Yet amongst the inmates, acknowledgement or the lack thereof can lead to some serious complications. Later on, I would learn about a practice called the "Prison Stare." It means, basically, that you have about three seconds to make an impression on a fellow inmate. It happens the very moment you encounter another inmate for the first time face to face. The first second you lock your gaze on his without a hint of smile or frown. Second two, you continue to hold your gaze without looking away. The third second is where you find out if you passed their inspection.

In my experience, men who are cowards or have something to hide cannot look another man in the eye. Honest men will stand tall and meet other men's gaze, with neither fear nor flinch. The first to look away is the weak one. Look too long though and you're challenging him to fight. And when you do look away, acknowledge the other man as you do it, or it will be taken as an affront and he will also challenge you to a fight. This unwritten code among the inmates was the same among the Marines of my day.

Men are always sizing up one another, and when a man cannot look you in the eye, he is either hiding something, not taking you seriously or is just plain blind. Luckily, as an employee, I would be exempt from the Prison Stare rule. We have a similar rule in the armed forces, just with less threat of imminent bodily injury. I've always made an effort to acknowledge other men, but the inmates and employees lived in separate worlds. And the laws that govern those worlds do not cross over.

"And where do you think you're going?" boomed a guard's voice. I was so lost in thought that I had somehow wandered off course.

"I'm sorry," I answered the guard, who stared down at me from the second-run (tier) balcony. "I must have taken a wrong turn. Where is the—"

"Who are you?" It was more of a demand than a question.

"My name is James Humphries. I'm the new art teacher."

"All education personnel must report to the education building for duty. Do you know where that is?"

"Yes, sir, yes I do. I just got a little—"

"Then you should be on your way."

That was another thing I was going to have to deal with: the security. Everything and everyone at a prison is accounted for at all times. You cannot simply just take a stroll through the cellblocks without ever being seen. Everyone has their place and purpose, and the same applies to wandering art teachers. I made it back to familiar territory, and after a series of turns and more concrete hallways, I had finally found my place at Ferguson.

My new art room was large, dusty, and in complete disarray. All I had were some bulky cabinets and prison tables ravaged by scratches and scribbling that resembled graffiti, not to mention an afternoon class already on my schedule. It was unforgettable, that moment when my first group of felons entered the room. One by one, they quietly took their seats. No one cast me a hardened stare or scornful glance. They just sat at their desks, looking glum.

Most of them were quite young, just as Dr. Lane Murray had described. There I was, full of anxiety over teaching these supposedly ruthless criminals, but that first group turned out to be nothing but a timid group of young men. The same look can be seen on the faces of new Marine recruits as they exit the bus to boot camp, a look even I had worn when I stepped on to base grounds on Paris Island in 1953.

To better understand who and what I was dealing with, I allowed the first week of classes to simply happen as if I was only observing. Once the guard had left the doorway, the men seemed to relax a little. After I introduced myself, which seemed totally pointless because none of them acknowledged me, they gradually began to rise up and fetch their work. Thought no actual art classes had been taught, inmates had been previously allowed to pursue small projects that were supervised by security personnel, not accredited art teachers.

It didn't take long before I noticed that my students already knew how to open the art cabinets to fish out supplies the instant my back was turned. Even though I stayed on high alert during every class, I soon learned that no amount of patrolling could deter inmate mischief.

One of my first challenges had to do with the design of the classroom. The size of the storage cabinets presented a security problem that needed fixing. My proud Scotch-Irish height of sixty-seven inches was no match for hulking cabinets that stretched up eight feet towards the ceiling. One row ran alongside the classroom's outer wall, effectively covering windows where outside guards could peer in. Another row ran up the middle the room, dividing the room into two separate but not equal sections. *Guess they haven't put much effort into classroom design,* I thought to myself.

I'm not a man who sits still when confronted by a problem, so I drafted a design for new cabinets that first week and assigned the task of building them to my exact specifications to the inmates in the woodworking shop. Soon I'd have shorter cabinets with better doors and tighter locks. Such a job could've taken a week in the free world but we were on prison time here: It only took two days for the inmates to finish the cabinets.

My teaching style had to evolve as well. A drawing demonstration for a single student couldn't last more than a few minutes, so I opted for class demonstrations. Mischievous high school teens I could handle, and I never had to worry about whether Jimmy was going to shank Bobby or even me! But having to secure myself against the possibility of bodily harm was new, so I asked the closest security guard to include my room on his regular rounds. This, however, got me nowhere.

"C'mon buddy. You must be new here," scoffed the guard. I didn't know if that was a "yes" or "go to hell," but at least I was trying to make the best of things. Sure, my classroom was isolated, in a prison, full of things that could be made to gouge a man, and not on the duty's regular circuit but . . . oh well . . . at least it had great natural light!

That first week also introduced me to the regimen of inmate life. Twice a day, the students were interrupted from their work for morning or afternoon prison count. All activity on in the unit stopped until the count was cleared. Class times changed every time an incident took place; for instance, whenever an inmate attempted to escape, the school shut down and all the teachers were sent home. The prison teachers knew our situation was unique. We didn't have the luxury of substitutes to cover for us when we fell ill. These were just facts of prison life.

Going to school is mandatory for all inmates housed by TDC, until they're either forty-five years old or a graduate from Windham's high school or GED program. Most students enjoyed their school days, because class was a lot easier than farm work. My class was unique because attendance was voluntary, so those who attended really wanted to be there. One student said to me, "In the streets, man, I was too busy to study. But now, I'm locked up, so school helps me pass the time."

Young Felons

In 1972, when I started at Ferguson, the average inmate there had a sixth grade education. The general population was a roughly forty percent

split between Anglos and African Americans, with Latinos as the remaining twenty percent. However, more Anglos and Latinos than African Americans consistently attended my art classes. Racial lines were invisibly drawn between the ethnic groups. I noticed that African Americans isolated themselves more often than any other group. Whether it was in the inmate-dining hall, during physical recreation or when attending movies, it didn't matter. They just kept to themselves. This did not seem to be any kind of outwardly enforced segregation, but a decision that they had made among themselves.

My students came from all walks of life and every social stratum. You just don't end up in a place like Ferguson, where most first-time felons do, for whistling in Sunday school. I soon found out that the offenses that my students had committed represented the extreme limits of criminal behavior. Many of their crimes had been gruesome, brutal and bereft from any sense of mercy or common decency.

These men had a separate set of rules they lived by, rules revolving around a code of the streets. Usually an inmate had some absurd rationalization that justified his crime, as he made every effort to blame anyone but himself. The men I met during those first weeks at Ferguson had a little or no sense of obligation to society. They felt entitled to whatever material means that they could acquire. In short, they lived by a value system that mirrored society's values in all the wrong ways.

The Paperboy

On my first day of class, in my first group of students, there sat Milton, the paperboy from my old stomping grounds in the Garden Oaks neighborhood of Houston.

"Didn't you have a paper route down in Houston?" I asked.

He lowered his head: "Yes, sir. Sorry I couldn't deliver your newspaper anymore, sir, but I had a problem." I remembered Milton as being such a good kid, full of smiles and laughter, like all kids.

"Well, that's okay," I didn't want to get into the details of a student's case history. But apparently, that was the only verbal cue he needed to rattle off his story.

"You see, I had this heroin habit. And my dad, well, he's a doctor. A surgeon! I just couldn't tell him I was a junkie!" Looking down again, Milton continued: "He stopped sending me money when I got kicked out of college. Then I lost my job, my car and my girlfriend. When the little money I did have ran out, I got desperate. I figured I could rob that hamburger stand on 34th street, but the police got to me. Now my dad will never talk to me again!"

From Dobie High to Ferguson State

Also among my first group of prison students was Terry, one of my high school students from my teaching days back at Dobie High. Now here he was, no more than five years after he graduated, kept segregated in One Block because of his effeminate behavior.

"Hello, Mr. Humphries." Like Milton, Terry also looked ashamed to see me. "Didn't think I'd see you again, being locked up and all."

I felt another story coming on.

"My family kicked me out when I was still at Dobie. So I started stealing purses and forging checks just to get by. But what else could I do? I was seventeen and sleeping on the street!" Nervously he looked at me and asked again, *"What else could I do?"*

Terry had been a good student in high school, one who had never given me any problems. Seeing him there caught me totally by surprise, so all I could do was muster a weak, "I don't know."

Back at Dobie, he'd always appeared anxious about leaving my class when the counselor called for him. Sometimes I'd see him sitting outside of her office, struggling with his internal beast. It had never occurred to me to ask him if he was having any problems, but now I knew.

Perhaps if the school, his parents, or even I, had tried harder to help, he would've never been arrested, expelled from Dobie High, and sent to Ferguson State.

So goes the adage: hindsight is always 20/20.

Barbara and Mary

Teaching for Windham was a unique experience, to say the least. I felt humbled working among the experienced teachers on the staff, people who had worked for years in the prison system. Most of the staff kept to themselves around a new hire, leaving me to fend for myself. Lucky for me, two wonderful special education teachers at Ferguson, Barbara Lindsay and Mary Oliphant, both aided me along my journey into the world of the Texas incarcerated. Soon I realized the goals of my art program and their curriculum were closely related, because both of our disciplines enabled students to employ their talents and abilities through positive reinforcement.

I became almost convinced Mrs. Oliphant had been teaching since before Moses brought the children of Israel out of Egypt. Not because she was the oldest, though she could have had a decade or two on me, but because she was the wisest. Her patience was another thing I admired, for she spent every day working tirelessly to encourage and praise her students, while still finding the time to advise a rookie like me.

"Never turn your back on your students," she would kindly say. "What they can get into, they *will* get into . . . and then some! Oh, and always be prepared to give positive advice whenever asked."

"Understood, Mrs. Oliphant."

"And, Mr. Humphries," she continued, "just be yourself. These men here can smell a fake."

Her friendship was also my introduction to the African American community of Huntsville. It was as though she had one hand on my shoulder guiding me, and her other on the Rock of Ages.

Barbara Lindsay also had a sublime way of inspiring her students to embrace an "of-course-you-can-do-it" kind of attitude. When all that encapsulated suffering seemed like it would drown us in despair, her delightfully positive and caring outlook on life brightened the day. With her radiant joy, Barbara helped keep both of our beasts at bay.

High Riders

I had spent one too many lunches in my humid classroom before I realized the officer's dining hall had Ferguson's most reliable air conditioner. But eating in such temperate bliss required every diner to buy a meal ticket. Even those who brought their own lunch to the dining room had to ante up the two and a half bucks for a ticket.

One afternoon, I peered through my classroom's heavily barred windows and spotted piles of white clothing and field boots in the field. Behind the mess sat a group of tattooed men, lounging completely naked in the little bit of noon hour's shade that was available. Lunch was everyone's time to relax, even for the inmates.

Washing up for lunch was another story. There was only one staff lavatory at the hall. It had one toilet, one sink, and terrible ventilation. During my first week I wondered why everyone would rush over to that little restroom just before lunchtime. Even normally polite guards would elbow their way through to get a good spot in line. Teachers literally sprinted from their classrooms at the first sign their students were in a guard's custody.

"Why is everyone in such a rush?" I asked one guard as he jogged by.

"High Riders!" he panted between strides.

"What is a—" I started to say, but he was already too far away to hear me. I wasn't in any hurry, so me and my coffee mug took our time walking over to the chow hall. That's when I arrived to quite a scene and learned why it was good idea to wash up before the High Riders got there. It wasn't because they were mean. No, some of them were the nicest guards at Ferguson. It was the incredible mess they left behind—a sight and stench that would rob any man of his appetite. In that modest lavatory, I found piles of sweaty gloves and sod-covered hats, along with bits of manure covering every surface, including the ceiling. Not exactly an appetite stimulant.

Don't get me wrong. I really admired the Riders. They were the only guards allowed to wear cowboy hats, instead of the typical police style worn by building officers. You knew when they were in the building from the sound of their jingling spurs. Each Rider was armed with a pistol at his side and a rifle by his saddle. They spent hours in the sun, watching over their Hoe Squads (inmates who tilled the earth with garden hoes) from the backs of American mustangs.

The sweat darkening their blue-trimmed uniforms spoke of their sultry industry. Ferguson's High Riders were true cowboys, only they wrangled men instead of cattle.

Country Boy

Inmates prepared all the food at Ferguson, and it was usually pretty tasty. On one occasion, the "Special of the Day" was my favorite: homegrown, Texas T-bone steak, cooked to order. While waiting for my turn to order, I attempted to strike up a conversation with Todd, a young blond field officer standing in front of me.

"You live 'round here?" I asked.

Todd snapped his eyes at me as if suddenly aware of my presence, stared for three seconds, then slowly nodded. "Yessir," he answered in thick East Texas accent. "I'm a country boy and I'm damn proud of it!"

I took the hint and left him alone. We had never spoken before—and it was the last time I'd see him alive.

The way I heard it later, Todd got into an argument with his wife that very night. No one knew what it was about. It could have been anything from dirty socks on the floor to an unpaid utility bill, but whatever it was it apparently got out of hand. When he decided to leave the house to cool off, his wife had a different solution in mind—she picked up a loaded deer rifle and filled his back full of buckshot. There were no witnesses, so most of the story could only be left to conjecture. Lucky for the wife, she was "no-billed" by a grand jury.

How quickly the beast can reach out anywhere, even to destroy a family. All it takes is easy access to firearms around a home and a brief moment of irrational behavior to take a human life. I only connected with the young man for a few moments, but I'll never forget the self-assurance and confidence of that country boy, and how he was so damn proud of it.

Esprit De Corps

The Windham program was in its third year when I arrived. Before Windham, only a limited education program existed, chiefly funded from Education and Recreation (E&R) Department monies earned from various sources, which included the annual Texas Prison Rodeo. But since inmate education was a low priority, many of our staffers had a low level of motivation. We had many of what I like to call "nine-to-five ghosts." We all work with these people. They're the ones who just want the paycheck. No one knows anything about their lives, before or after working hours. They just show up, clock in, complain all day, clock out, and then—*poof*—they disappear, like a ghost.

When I started at Ferguson, I intentionally ate my lunch with security personnel instead of the teachers. They were responsible for my safety, so I felt like I needed to know them better. I was raised in Mississippi, which helped me to understand their local value system. In the Deep South, the term "redneck" refers to a respectable rural person who works hard in the outdoor sun. A redneck's values are close to the earth and anchored in his faith in God. He has a strong sense of community, and knows the virtue of hard work. A meaningful education is encouraged, whether it requires public or home schooling, so as long as it prepares a child for their place on the family farm.

Some of Ferguson's officers had never been further south than New Waverly, further west than Anderson, further north than Madisonville, or further east than Livingston. But I respected their outlook and tried to see things from their perspective. On the flipside, the higher-ranking officers were as well traveled and educated as anyone I knew.

My military and Mississippi background helped me develop a spirit of cooperation for my art program. The Marine Corps taught me to value the motivational force of the human spirit, as expressed through their "Esprit de Corps," and to value the counsel of my senior officers. To this day, I believe in the Marine Corps statement: "The difficult we do now, the impossible just takes a little longer." Teaching art here, I knew, would just have to take a little longer.

Mystery Meat

The prison cafeteria menu was always an adventure in federally funded gastronomy. Because Windham offered a culinary arts class, the employees had the honor of being guinea pigs for all of their creations. Most of the meat dishes served throughout TDC deserved their inmate-given monikers, names like "Ferguson's Mystery Meat" and "Ellis Unit's Dynamite Chicken."

American meat loaf is just ground beef, various spices, and portions of leftovers. Oh, and ketchup. Because the ingredients are ground up and blended, other protein products can be added if available or so desired. All our ground meat originated from TDC prison farms, or a well-to-do hunter or fisherman. Because there's no way to be sure of the meat's origin, that's where the mystery begins.

One day, the inmates served up an especially distinctive yet peculiar meatloaf. It was light in color, with an unusually smooth texture, and a flavor that was simply indescribable. It smelled different too. So different, that I had to ask Andy, the officer in charge in the kitchen, to explain.

"Remember that bass fishing tournament at Lake Livingston last weekend?" Andy replied. "Well, the contestants donated their catch to our culinary arts class. We decided not to cook the fish as a fish dish, and instead add to it some pork and chicken and so we made meat loaf."

"What do you call it?" I asked.

"I don't have the foggiest idea, but is sure tastes good!"

"So, it's really a 'mystery meat' then."

"Ha," he chuckled, "I kind of like that. Sure fits the situation!"

I also couldn't resist calling their venison meatloaf "The Road Kill Special." It just fit.

But then I heard a rumor that permanently killed my appetite for all meat loaf. One day, the story went, an inmate working in the meat processing facility miraculously vanished. The whole unit was on lockdown for more than two days, but the guards never found a trace of him. He helped prepare meat alongside one of those big, industrial-grade grinders, the kind of machine big enough for a man to fall into and never be heard from again. I don't know if the kitchen staff was yanking my chain with that story, and today I still don't know. But one thing is for sure: Every scrap of meat that entered that grinder ended up in the meat loaf.

Tarantulas Among Us

The food at Ferguson's inmate chow hall wasn't what anyone would call great until the day the Chef arrived from the Ellis Unit. Before prison, the Chef had tried his hand at cooking the books for a ritzy hotel in Dallas, but, as he learned, he should've just stuck with cooking the guests' food. Now the State of Texas would make use of the services of a genuine *chef de cuisine* while he served time for felony embezzlement.

As soon as the Chef walked in the classroom door, I had to ask myself, "Okay, what's going on? What's this older inmate doing in my class?" He looked at least forty years old in a population where the median age was twenty-four.

"Howdy," he proudly announced. "They call me Chef, and I'm here from the Ellis Unit to improve all y'all's cooking. And when I found out there's an art class, well hell, I had to sign up!"

After the art supplies were distributed and the students were working away, I asked Chef, "So, what kind of artwork do you want to do?"

"Paintings," he exclaimed. "I want to paint real good paintings!"

"We can do that. Have you ever painted before?"

"Nope."

"Alright, then let's get started with some basic brush technique."

As I was demonstrating how to stretch a canvas, I prodded Chef for some more answers.

"So, about this food quality: Are you going to get better ingredients?"

"Nope."

"Okay, but how about the meat?"

"Same meat."

"Milk? Eggs? Grains?"

"All the same."

"Well, there's got to be something you're not telling me!" He just sat there looking smug, so I kept on. "You've got to have a special secret, like your own set of cooking pans. I've heard that all chefs have one knife that just does it all."

"Nope," he chuckled, "No secret knife. Besides, the hotel took that from me when I got caught. Nah, I have to use the same food, except I'm gonna show 'em how to cook it better. I might even bring you a sample of what I mean, Mr. Humphries. Then you can meet my tarantula."

"Your *what?*" I choked out.

"My pet tarantula," he repeated. "I bring him up sometimes for a visit. He gives me ideas for my dishes." And he wasn't joking.

The next day of class, Chef brought me a sample of his cake.

"Chef," I started, "this is absolutely delectable!" Good food cannot be truly enjoyed while standing up, so I took a seat at my desk and lost myself in gastronomical delight of his cooking.

"And with the same stuff as before, just made right this time," Chef said while standing behind me. He sounded happy that I liked it . . . in fact, almost a little too happy. That's when I noticed that the entire class was smiling. *Inmates never smile, Jim!* Then I remembered Mrs. Oliphant's sage advice: "Never turn you back on an inmate." Too late! I was so entranced by his culinary competence that I forgot to keep Chef in my sights when I sat down. When I turned back to face

Chef, I came eyeball to multiple-eyeball with a black, hairy tarantula, calmly sitting on his forearm. It scared the living daylights out of me, but I couldn't panic. Rumor has it that spiders can sense fear.

"Will it bite?" I asked, trying to keep my voice from squeaking.

"Only if it thinks it needs to," he answered with another chuckle. "They're all over this part of Texas but come out only after sundown. That's when they like to move around."

The spider wasn't doing much moving, just lurking and staring at me. I slowly pushed my chair away to a more comfortable distance.

"Oh, don't let his little size fool you," Chef warned. "I've seen him jump on a man ten feet away."

Great. Just great, I thought.

He gently stroked his pet and added, "Some say they can sense fear. That's when they pump their bodies up and down, like doing

pushups. He's not doing that now, so you're okay. He just lies around most of the time. Here, do you want to hold him?"

I managed to get out a quick "Uh, no thank you. He looks quite comfortable right where he is."

He laughed again, and then asked to be excused to his cell. "Be my guest," I told him. As he left, one thing kept bothering me: I didn't see him bring in the tarantula nor did I see him leave with it. Every inmate was routinely searched when they left the art area, so where in the hell did he hide that thing?

That was my first encounter with East Texas arachnids. Tarantulas seemed to be everywhere in Huntsville. Every day at sundown, dozens of them would cross the road in front of my house, where I was living alone after my divorce. The spiders would crawl up the driveway, through my carport, and on to the edge of the forest behind my property. At first I tried to exterminate them. My cats also waged battle alongside me, whacking them with their paws, but alas we fought in vain. Every evening, more regiments of tarantulas marched on through my carport and into the Texas woods.

Eventually, I just gave up the fight. Soon after, my cats ignored them, too. That was when a forest ranger told me I lived in an area where you can find 5,000 different types of spider per acre! He speculated that my house had been built along a path that the tarantulas had been following for ages. Concrete driveway or not, they were here before I was, so, the ranger informed me, I had better learn to live with them.

"Y'all just keep to the driveway and out of my house," I called out one night to the evening's battalion of tarantulas as it scuttled by. "I don't want any uninvited guests just checking in! If y'all can do that, my cats and I will let you carry on, unmolested across my property." My neighbors likely thought I was crazy, standing in my driveway talking to a bunch of spiders, but I was serious. In fact, I even made a miniature yellow diamond sign with a tarantula's silhouette and the words "Tarantula XING," and planted it at the end of my driveway.

.38 Special

Eventually, the time came when the Texas Education Agency (TEA) would pay a visit to Ferguson to review the progress of the educational program. One day, after almost a year of piloting the art program, a TEA representative named George decided to observe my class. Since our program was funded directly from the state legislature, disappointing the bureaucrats was not an option.

Earlier that day, Anse, one of my students, had asked for a few simple materials: an X-acto knife, ruler, pencil, watercolor brush, white Bristol board, Elmer's Glue, and two ounces of black ink. I usually made a habit of constantly circulating among my students to discourage any form of mischief, but that day I was busy impressing my TEA visitor. And, as time went on, things seemed to be going very smoothly. The students were busy working on projects, leaving me free to show off their talents.

Anse spent the better half of every class arguing with the others about who was the more qualified handgun expert. But that day he remained quiet, sparing the class his usual sermon on his favorite Smith & Wesson. Instead, he was busily working with all those supplies he requested. That's when Mrs. Oliphant's warning popped into my head again. "What they can get into, they *will* get into!"

Right before lunch hour, George, the TEA representative, and I were standing and talking together. Behind him, I saw Anse rise from his workspace and start to slowly stroll toward us with both hands hidden behind his back. I knew he was up to something, but it was already too late. The next few seconds all happened in slow motion: As the inmate closed in, he drew his hand from behind his back: It held a black .38 Special snub nose, leveled right at our heads. *"That's a gun he's got pointed at us,"* I thought. *"We're going to be gunned down in my art class by some crazy MacGyver of Ferguson!"* Then he pulled the trigger.

"BOOM!" he roared. I stood dumbfounded. George went white and almost fainted. No smoke, no pearly gates. *It was a fake and we were still alive!*

"Gotcha!" He threw his head back and broke into bellowing laughter, tears streaming down his face. I snatched the paper pistol away, stormed out to the door and immediately called for a guard. Yeah, he had gotten the best of me, made a mockery of my class and probably cost me my job . . . but still, I couldn't help being proud of him. I've seen plenty of .38 Specials, yet never one so perfectly reproduced from scratch. He had combined paper mâché and origami masterfully, two techniques I still hadn't taught anyone yet. I felt both extremely impressed and terribly embarrassed that his pistol was a perfect example of the quality of art an inmate could produce.

Doing my best not to cringe, I escorted the now speechless TEA representative out of my class and left him in the care of a more vigilant guard. I hurried over to Mr. Grogan, our principal at time, to show him the paper gun.

"He made this using just paper and glue," I reported as I laid the gun on the principal's desk.

"Wow. That's some good stuff. Looks . . . real!" Understandably, Mr. Grogan was also surprised. "But how did he get the time to make this? You're not teaching inmates this kind of stuff, are you?"

"No, sir, of course not," I assured him.

"You know what? Save it for the Education and Recreation (E&R) director. Let's go, Mr. Humphries."

As we walked into the office of Mr. Keegan, the E&R director, I thoughtlessly brandished the pistol and announced, "Director, we've got a problem!" In one motion, Mr. Keegan looked up and leaped backward, kicking over his chair.

"Relax," Mr. Grogan broke in. "Look here, it's only made from paper."

"Paper?" the director asked, the color now returning to his cheeks as he studied the pistol. "And where in the hell did an inmate get the time to make this?" Now I was in for it.

Mr. Keegan stood glaring at me as we explained, stretching out every second of tension, but I stood firm and readied myself for the consequences.

"Mr. Humphries," he finally started, now in a calmer tone of voice, "since you are still a little wet behind the ears, I'll let this one slide. But only this one time! This art program is still new, so we can't give the warden any reason to pull the plug. Paper gun or not, this cannot happen again, understood?"

"Yes, sir!" Dodged the bullet this time. "My apologies, sir."

"Okay. Now, if you don't mind." Mr. Keegan gestured towards the door for us to leave (and you bet I was the first one out). But before we were out of earshot, he added one last piece of advice:

"And Jim, next time you feel the need to burst into my office and pull a gun on me, please give me the courtesy of doing it *after* lunch."

"Sorry, sir."

For his little joke, my student Anse enjoyed solitary confinement for three days and was banned from art class. Not surprisingly, it's against the law for an inmate to make a fake weapon. But he couldn't have been happier. He'd proved himself to be Ferguson's uncontested pistol expert and his proof would later be displayed at a Texas Prison Museum.

Through the following months, George visited my class several times. We never forgot the paper pistol incident, nor did we talk about it. It was simply too extraordinary to relive. The other teachers couldn't understand why he liked to chat with me while he just evaluated them. What they did not know was that we had something in common: the unspoken bond two men share when they both have the same near-death experience. Whether hoaxed or not, the feeling of mortality in that moment was real.

Catatonic Redhead

The vacancy caused by Anse's departure brought a new student to my class. At first he didn't speak at all, so I called him Red. He sported the typical short-cropped crew cut of a Marine Corps recruit. A pale, freckled complexion and reddish brown teeth, stained from years of tobacco chew, complimented his vermillion hair, but it was his haunted eyes that left the most striking impression. They stared through you, not at you.

After Mrs. Oliphant brought Red to me, she pulled me to one side and whispered, "Jim, Principal Grogan suggested you try to work with this young man before we have him evaluated for possible commitment to the treatment center."

"What do you know about him?" I asked.

"We have no record of any education. He's scored a zero on every form of test that's been given, but appears free of any mental deficiency."

"That's odd." I took another look at him, looking for a sign of life. "And he's always like this?"

"I'm afraid so," she answered. "He just sits around and stares into space, like no one exists. Jim, he won't speak!"

"Where is he from?"

"Big Thicket. It's not too far from here."

"Okay, I'll see what I can do."

In some ways, Red looked like the hundreds of other young, first-time offenders at the Ferguson Unit: white uniform, black shoes and belt, hair shaved short. When I saw their regulation haircuts during my first tour of the unit, I commented about it to Warden Collins and Dr. Murray.

"I feel at home here!" I said. They both looked at me puzzled, somewhat surprised by my candor. *Time for some quick damage control, Jim.* "These young men and their shaved heads remind me of the young boots at Paris Island."

Their expressions relaxed. Then, Dr. Murray said, "Well, that explains the tattoos on your arms."

"Yes, ma'am." I had a Marine Corps emblem tattooed on my left shoulder to honor my country and a rose with a dagger stabbed through it on my right forearm to honor my ex-wife.

Other TDC employees often told me my students felt more comfortable with me because of my tattoos. To my inmate students, tattoos expressed a willingness of an individual to endure pain in order to express something of value. Tattoos were not a fashion accessory like they are today. In 1972, mostly men had tattoos and most of those who did were criminals or soldiers.

By Texas law, inmates had to go to school one day a week until they obtained a high school diploma or GED. The balance of their time was spent in some form of work: farm, industrial, clerical, or maintenance. Texas Correctional Industries is a large and very complex enterprise benefiting many public institutions, hospitals and schools. From license plates to school desks to bars of soap, inmates provide an invaluable source of goods that everyone in our society benefits from.

One of the worse things that can happen to an inmate is losing the privilege of going to work or school. Being locked down in your cell is only a few steps above solitary confinement. Since Red couldn't work in his condition, I requested that he be allowed to attend school daily. Every student was offered different drawing media, including crayons, Ebony pencils, charcoal and Grumbacher pastels, depending on their level of motor skills and behavioral control. So Red got the crayons.

As I began to demonstrate drawing techniques, he continued to sit and stare blankly at the paper. I tried placing crayons near his hands, asking him to pick the color he liked best. I began making random marks with each color, hoping to get him thinking about the crayon color and see what it looked like on the piece of paper. Eventually, he picked up a green crayon and scribbled: my first breakthrough!

His motor skills, awareness, and acceptance of his environment gradually increased after the first week. In the weeks that followed, he progressed rapidly, indicating an interest for painting pastel portraits. By the end of week three, he was painting portraits, communicating verbally, and making friends with other students. His self-esteem had greatly improved, so I asked him if he was ready to be retested.

"Yes," he replied enthusiastically.

Red scored at a solid sixth grade level, which was the norm for the overall prison population. Because of his test scores, he could enroll in a vocational program. The next time I saw him, he was working a drill press in the machinist shop. He stopped working the moment he noticed me, and with a happy grin, waved a brown-gloved hand my way.

For the moment, he'd pushed his beast back into darkness. His catatonia had not been brought on by schizophrenia but by an intense fear of being locked away in prison. I would learn later how just lucky he had been when I found out what happened to those inmates whom the prison system considered dysfunctional: Most were committed to the Psychiatric Treatment Center, located at the main Huntsville Unit. To fail society and be sent to prison is one thing, but to fail at being a prisoner and then be committed to the Psychiatric Treatment Center was an entirely different situation.

My success with Red attracted the attention of Ferguson's resident psychologist. He approached me in a kind but direct manner, asking if I would consider piloting an art therapy program at the Huntsville Unit's Psychiatric Treatment Center.

"What you did with that inmate is nothing short of remarkable, given his quick recovery."

"Thank you, but it was nothing really," I answered. "All I did was give him the tools to express himself."

"A humble man," said the psychologist. "I like that. Say, would you like to try this out on a whole class? We have a treatment facility at Walls, and I can tell you there are plenty of patients who could benefit from your approach."

"You really think I can help them?"

"Not just me but others too, know about your student's progress. Mrs. Oliphant brought it to the attention of Principal Grogan, who in turn told the Warden. When I got wind of it, I made a few phone calls and found out Huntsville wants you."

"Okay then," I replied. "I'll do it."

By then, I was taking anything that helped fill up the hours after work. My house, located on the edge of Huntsville, was empty and lonesome. There, amid the residue of a divorce settlement, I faced my own beast, born of loneliness and self-doubt. I'd hoped the pieces of my personal life would begin to fit together again as I became more involved at Ferguson. Every day when I went to work, I was forced to keep my personal problems outside of the prison fence. Upon entering the prison grounds, I would quietly repeat the phrase, "I'm okay and you're okay," as a sort of mantra to soothe my troubled soul.

After only a few months at Ferguson, I now worked second assignment, in addition to my regular work. Nothing could have prepared me for what would happen at the Treatment Center because, to my knowledge, by 1973 art therapy for Texas inmates had never been attempted. The afternoon drive to the Huntsville Unit would be an uneventful twenty miles down FM 247. Four o'clock was too late for red bird suicide flights and too early for tarantulas crossing the road.

HUNTSVILLE:
THE WALLS UNIT

The Treatment Center

THE FIRST MONDAY AFTERNOON I walked into the Huntsville Unit marked the beginning of a long association with the oldest prison in the state of Texas. The locals called it the "Walls Unit" after its enormous, dark-red brick walls that towered over the neighboring streets. The walls were thirty feet tall and three feet thick. Towers housed guards at every corner, each armed with a .357 Magnum, an M16 semiautomatic rifle and a shotgun. No firearms are allowed inside any Texas prison, unless extreme circumstances warranted. Such a circumstance arose in 1974 during the eleven-day Carrasco siege, when the Texas Rangers joined with Walls Unit guards in ending one of the longest prison hostage standoffs in U.S. history (a story I'll tell later).

The Walls Unit had little in common with the Ferguson Unit. The oppressive red bricks surrounding the facility robbed the inside of its natural light, lending to its onerous atmosphere. Walls Unit was where all executions in Texas were carried out, another morbid fact of prison life. After you passed through the first sliding electric door, the passage to the normal visitors' area during weekends was to the left. Women had to check their purses with a guard, even after being examined by the Radio Picket. Another passage led to the prison barbershop, where for a small annual fee, an employee could get a haircut from an inmate trustee barber. Past the entrance to the warden's office sat the warden's secretary Adrienne, the original Steel Magnolia and the biggest Dallas Cowboys fan I ever met.

Continuing forward, I passed under a guard in a metal cage suspended from the ceiling: the Swinging Picket. The Swinging Picket controlled the two doors of a floor-to-ceiling brass bar enclosure: the Bull Ring. Just like the small enclosure used to mount buckaroos on bulls at rodeos, the Bull Ring was the last safe point between the prison and the free world. As I stood in the Bull Ring, I realized: *Someone other than myself controls my movements in prison*; a fact all employees had to accept.

As I passed through the Bull Ring, I spotted a row of desks to the left of me. Each desk was split down the middle by a heavy sheet of plexiglass that separated each side from the other. Sitting on one side of the glass would be the closest an inmate at Walls would be to the free world. They could see and speak with their visitors or attorneys, but never actually touch them. To be robbed of life's most simple human interactions, like the sympathetic touch from someone who loves you, is yet another form of incarceration a convict must endure.

On my right side was the transient inmate holding area, where inmates waited for a Chain Bus to take them to another prison or medical facility. These inmates all looked to be clutching white laundry bags containing a few personal items tightly to their sides, along with a small, but very precious, electric fan. Floor-to-ceiling brass bars separated the employee passage through the Bull Ring from the other two sections. As I heard the first brass bar door snap shut, the second door began to open. With another deep breath, I stepped into the world of the Walls Unit.

Directly to the left of the Bull Ring was the entrance to the oldest portion of the Walls: East Wing. Built in 1848, it existed during the notorious outlaw era of the Old West. Here, gunslingers like John Wesley Hardin and the Kiowa warrior White Bear served their time. East Wing has the oldest cells in the Walls Unit, and because it is also adjacent to the old death row wing and execution chamber, none of the inmates wanted to be housed there. Many believed East Wing was haunted by the ghosts of executed men.

I soon came upon the building officer's desk. There I presented my identification to a middle-aged guard by the name of Major Murdock, and politely asked for directions to the treatment center.

The Major inspected me for a moment, pushing his hat further back on his head while locking his eyes on me. With just that one look, he'd sized me up, apparently deciding that I was worthy of his time. He grabbed the phone and gave an order: "Send an employee to the building officer's desk to escort Mr. James Humphries to the treatment center!"

In time, I learned that every employee, officer and inmate quickly responded to the Major's voice. Major Murdock was an officer respected by everyone, and for good reason.

He was tough yet reasonable, with a sense of humor few individuals were privileged to know.

The psychologist I had met at Ferguson arrived shortly thereafter to lead the way to the Huntsville Psychiatric Treatment Center. As we entered the prison courtyard, immediately to the left was the chapel, built to look like a small church. On the south side of the chapel were various types of weight lifting equipment: benches, squat racks and several free weights. Further to the left was the large white structure of the prison hospital and in the northeast corner of the courtyard was the entrance to death row and the location of Old Sparky, the infamous Texas electric chair now on display in the Texas Prison Museum. Not even the guards took liberty near this area, for the atmosphere there was eerie. The beast had claimed too many victims in those cells and in that chair.

We passed the stairs leading down to the officers' dining hall and a concrete ramp that ran up first to the inmate dining hall, and then continued along to the top level where the education building and inmate law library and were situated. The odor of that day's mystery meat reminded me it was near time for supper. Inmates filed into the chow hall, leaving the courtyard deserted. Empty of people, the prison courtyard echoed with sharp sounds bouncing off the brick walls and concrete floor: the sound of plates sliding onto barbells, blended with the clacking of dominoes on recreation tables. These would be the first signs that supper had ended. I had to stop and stand still for a moment to absorb the sounds and the sights of this vast correctional institution.

"Mr. Humphries, we had better get a move on," said the psychologist, snapping me out of my artist's trance. "I'm hungry too, but we still have to introduce you to more of the staff."

"Sorry. I was having a moment."

"Hmmm, well you won't have time to have many of those in here. Walls ain't no joke and neither is this: Five Building, home of the treatment center. And your new home."

He led me through a small door into the multi-leveled Five Building. I began to sense an ominous presence as we climbed up the metal stairs to the third-floor enclosed metal walkway that led to the treatment center. We briefly stopped at the office of Major Herriage, the officer in charge of the treatment center, to explain the purpose of my program. The major said he and his staff would be happy to cooperate, which was music to my ears. During the next four years working at the treatment center, I would always receive the utmost in courtesy, respect and cooperation from all of the staff.

We left the major's office and proceeded through an enclosed metal catwalk. The run was aloft three floors, high enough to keep personnel safe. Below us was the patients' recreation yard and outdoor movie theater. There, inmates enjoyed movies and even a rare music concert.

As we walked along, I continued to sense an ominous presence. Describing this is difficult for me, because it's a vibration I could feel but not on my skin. It was a sound I heard but not with my ears. For my entire life, I've received impressions that simply could not be explained. They would just happen, as if I could see into the future or into the depths of a person's soul. My impressions appeared in various forms, such as emotions or thoughts or visualizations. On occasion, I've received precise premonitions that would almost always come true. I had to accept these impressions as a type of intuition, a gift I never shared with anyone outside of my closest family and friends.

In teaching and relationships, people usually noted my sensitivity and empathy toward others. Most considered my empathy to be an asset to my profession, but they never learned about the depth of this empathy. I hoped my ominous feeling during that first walk into the treatment center was just the nervous anticipation of a new teaching situation, but my gut told me there would be much more to it than that.

At the Ferguson Unit, I taught in a classroom; here, things were completely different. Those housed in the treatment center had to be under round-the-clock care, so I was never too far from other staff. Since there were no formal classrooms in the center, classes would be taught in the middle of the patients' cellblock. Two runs surrounded the class area where two massive recreational tables sat bolted to the floor of the cellblock. Each tabletop was made of a thick and cold concrete slab, supported by a heavy steel construction. Vertical windows stretching up two stories furnished the only natural light to the center of the treatment center.

Everything about A-Block lacked warmth, even while the Texas sun warmed the outside. I kept my blazer buttoned in a futile effort to ward off the constant chill, but it is hard to put into words how lifeless the air felt. The floor was a bare concrete gray. All surfaces were painted a dull shade of institutional green or TDC gray. This place was not like Ferguson, or anything else at Walls for that matter. With its dozens of cells housing the most psychologically disturbed inmates in all of Huntsville, A-Block left an impression on me that I never could forget.

Through a small window with thick, musty glass, I watched as my first students slowly trundled out from their cells, prodded along their way by cautious guards. After the prescribed eight were seated, an outside guard cranked the door. Steel cables and wheel bearings sang in a hissing exhalation, which ended in the heavy metallic downbeat of numerous doors closing in concert. Armed with white mounting boards, twenty-pound duplicator paper, manila folders, and a cigar box full of Crayola crayons, I entered A-Block to pioneer the first art therapy program for inmates in the State of Texas.

Blue Bird

"Mr. Humphries, your students are ready," called out a guard.

As I walked inside A-Block, a hush swept over the cells. It felt as if every eye in every cell was fixed on me. A quick glance around confirmed that I was right. Some inmates were staring. Others were motioning to me with arms and hands dangling beyond their cell bars, beckoning me to come closer.

Several inmate patients on the upper run of the cellblock were rapidly pacing back and forth, muttering incoherent words. Others made gestures as if they were fighting back some invisible attacker. One patient flushed the toilet every time he completed a pacing cycle inside his cell. I watched him stare transfixed at the water funneling down the drain, lost in his own psychosis. Their clumsy gestures, relentless pacing, and occasional exhortations could be likened to that of a caged beast trapped in its own private hell.

Green-shirted hospital workers administered medication, uninterested in my presence. Small paper cups filled with pills were handed to each patient through shoebox-size openings. Only then, during that brief encounter with the staff, did the men come back to reality. Each patient had to open his mouth to show the hospital worker that he had swallowed the medication. And all complied in robotic fashion.

As I approached my students with my crayons and drawing papers, they showed no facial expression, no movement of anticipation. They just sat motionless, like statues in white jumpsuits, staring into nothingness. Having no idea how an art therapist worked with the insane, all I could rely upon was my intuition, teaching experience, and if things got hairy, my Marine Corps training.

The sixty minutes of that first session felt like an eternity. My students never made eye contact and never spoke. Each student failed miserably at following all directions. Some just gave up and stared at the paper. *How am I supposed to teach art to these men! They're not half alive, they're half dead!* Flustered, I took liberty from trying and surveyed my sorry excuse for an art class. From the beginning, I knew they were not the problem. I was the wrong man for this job.

How naïve had I been, thinking that these men, whose minds were on the brink of collapse, held together by only a psychotropic cocktail of barbiturates and neuroleptics, could learn at the pace of, well, any sane person. They were doing the best they could with what they had, so if I was going to make any sort of headway, I needed to alter my approach.

I thought it necessary to keep the instructional objective very simple, so I thought if I showed them pictures cut from magazines, they could draw what they saw. Oh, what a mistake that was! I decided to hand one student a picture of a blue jay and a blue crayon, but that just turned into a massive ordeal. He gripped the crayon so firmly he could have crushed it. What happened to that poor crayon was so far from anything I had seen in all my years as an artist.

With the palm of his hand, the inmate pushed the crayon onto the surface of the paper, crushing it into a pile of blue bits. As he squinted through black horn-rimmed glasses, sweat trickled down his face as he tried to make sense of the blue jay in the picture. Then he grabbed another blue crayon and smashed that one into bits on the paper. *"I'm going to run out of all my blue if this keeps up,"* I thought.

I looked at my other students for some sign of hope, but they all were sitting motionless after their own feeble attempt to draw their subject. It felt like being suspended in another dimension. I had demonstrated what to do and encouraged them to pick a picture of their choice, but the class was grinding to a halt. We were dead in the water and sinking fast! That was when I took a really good look at them. Up until that moment, I was concerned most with getting them to do what I instructed, but then it dawned on me just who I was teaching.

Objectivity is completely beyond them at the moment, Jim, I thought. Then I heard the chuckling from the observing guards and realized I was speaking these thoughts out loud. I sneered back at them. There

I was floundering with this mad group of misfits, and all they were doing was standing idling by, enjoying the show.

One student, named Ted, who was trying to draw the bird, looked to be in his late teens. He was most likely a first-time offender from Ferguson. He stood over six and a half feet tall, with a prominently high and rectangular forehead and short black hair. His pale white skin blended with the white prison hospital jumpsuit. Black horn-rimmed glasses framed narrow eyes that were always focused somewhere beyond the cellblock.

Suddenly Ted stood up and yelled, "I want to go to my house now!" (As a general rule, the treatment personnel replaced the word "cell" with "house," and "inmate" with "patient" to lessen the trauma of incarceration.) A drooling elderly patient in front of him also stood up. Then gradually, they all stood up and faced toward their cells. The security guard, who had been laughing during the entire proceedings, walked over to them, smirking in my direction. He led them away, prodding them as they shuffled back to their cells.

Afterward, the guard, still smirking, approached me: "Our psychologists would like a word with you before you leave."

Change in Plans

"Jim, we have a new direction for your work," Dr. Gores, one of the treatment center's two psychiatric doctors told me. They instructed that I read the medical and social history of each of my inmate students, and keep individual records on their progress. The records would provide clinical psychologists of the Baylor College of Medicine in Houston invaluable insight into the minds of men experiencing trauma due to incarceration.

"I've heard you're having some struggles adjusting, but we want you to know your work here is important," he continued, "not only to our patients but to future patients and programs as well."

"I appreciate that," I answered. "Any direction you can give me will help."

"Maybe you can try a more cognitive approach," replied the other psychiatrist, Dr. Bennett. "These men have a faint idea of reality. Get them to tap into their fantasies, and you'll have a wellspring of opportunity to understand them."

"Are you suggesting that we work in a purely creative manner, with no more physical references to work from or copy?"

"That would be the ideal approach, Mr. Humphries."

"Okay then, I'll do it. They'll create art from their imaginations, with no interference from me."

"No, you can help them. But it's going to be touch and go for a while."

That got a chuckle from us all. "Yes, sir. To say the least."

"Glad to hear you're on board with the suggestion."

"How could I not be? We all saw the blue jay incident!" We chuckled again. "It was enough for me to consider throwing in the towel, but you two have given this project a new direction. Thank you, doctors."

Although my first class left me very discouraged, I was beginning to feel comfortable at the Walls Unit. After I left Five Building, the ominous vibrations ceased. I knew I was going to have to get used to it though. Then a thought occurred to me: being rejected from society and put in prison is one thing, but to be rejected *from the rejected*, is entirely something else. The best any of the patients could hope for was to become behaviorally stable enough to be put back into the general population. Not exactly something to look forward to.

Each day I left Five Building and entered the prison courtyard, the combined odors of hot chow coming from the dining halls made me wonder how much better their cooking might be from my own. I took my time walking through the courtyard: smelling the air, listening to the sound of plastic trays being washed in the inmate chow hall, accompanied by the metallic ringing of barbell plates.

As I approached the Bull Ring, I looked down to my left at the lower cellblock of East Building and saw two African American inmates enjoying a game of dominoes. The normal sounds of prison life contrasted to the stark cacophony of the treatment center. After the last door closed behind me, I stood for a moment on the front steps of the Walls and listened to the soft cooing of the resident pigeons. High overhead, the chimney swifts chirped and circled in small black swarms, preparing to bed down for the night in one of the tall, red brick chimneys of Walls Unit.

Take a deep breath, Jim. This is far from over.

Shadows of Depression

Darkness cloaked the edge of Big Thicket forest, the place where I lived alone on the outskirts of Huntsville. My divorce settlement had left me with a new but empty house, along with a nauseating loneliness. Recurring nightmares disturbed my sleep, and my depression began to press on my mind. I knew I had to do something to counter the swamp of despair I was sinking into, but I just didn't have the weapons to fight back my own beast. Fiercely, I began to lift weights and draw into the late hours of the night, between bouts of heavy drinking.

A favorite pastime of mine was drinking whole six packs of beer and then stacking the empty cans on the every windowsill in the house. Each time my friends visited, I made sure they too added their empty cans to my makeshift curtains. After months of drinking, I had every front window full of beer cans, blocking the outside sun while trapping me inside with my misery. Ironically, I too had built a Walls Unit of my own.

One morning I woke up, lying on my filthy, barren floor. The stench of empty beer cans and sweaty, unlaundered clothes turned my stomach. I struggled to my feet and plodded into the kitchen only to find a scene straight out of a B-rated horror film. There were tarantulas everywhere inside of my refrigerator, munching happily on what remained of my rancid leftovers. Apparently I had left the patio door, along with refrigerator, open all night. My head throbbed, my back ached, and my home just plain stank! Finally, I realized that this was rock bottom.

I knew then that in order to continue my work with the inmates at the treatment center, I had to have a handle on my own psyche. Partying with friends and drinking alcohol was not the answer. It only intensified the pain of loneliness and failure from my first marriage. Although I had been attending Sunday Mass at St. Thomas Catholic Church, I began to go to Daily Mass also. The fellowship at Daily Mass had a cleansing effect on my soul. There, I could leave the unanswered questions of my divorce and the suffering I witnessed every day at work before the Altar of Christ.

It was also then I realized something about me was changing. I was becoming acutely aware of the feelings of others around me. The spiritual debris of those forsaken prisoners had been clinging to my psyche, and it was polluting my soul. Church fellowship gave me energy to face the next day and cleansed me of the psychic toxins inadvertently left by the sad men I was trying in earnest to inspire, teach, and rehabilitate.

Bondo Special

One morning, I was traveling on Texas State Highway 75 in my ancient dark green International Travelall. An elderly couple in their equally ancient Plymouth apparently needed to use the lane I was in at the exact moment I was occupying it. You can imagine what happened next: old couple merges without signaling, I slam on the brakes, slide sideways and avert total catastrophe with my amateur stuntman skills! Everyone escaped unscathed, save for my front left fender.

"Sorry, son," apologized the husband, "but my wife Eunice was driving, and she's never been good at piloting the Plymouth."

"Now you wait a damn minute," snapped Eunice. "If you had just bought that Ford, we'd never have problems. Plymouth doesn't take into account what a small woman needs to drive around! Henry, you know I can't see over this damn steering wheel!"

"Ma'am, don't worry about it," I interrupted. "The damage is not that bad. Plus, I can have my work fix it for next to nothing. And Henry, maybe you should think about trading in for a Ford next time this happens. Really, ma'am, sir, there's no problem."

Visibly pleased, Eunice gloated while Henry stamped his feet, still fuming from her foul-up. Before they could get another word in edgewise, I bid them good day and headed off to Ferguson State, where I hoped our auto body class would mend my Travelall's fender.

Apparently, no matter how knowledgeable or experienced we human beings become, there will always be a situation when we eat those famous last words: "No problem."

With great expectations, I made arrangements with the Windham Vocational Department. That was my first mistake. Because I was still new, I was unaware of the college-level auto body class also at Ferguson, which was taught after hours in the same space and on the same equipment as the daytime Windham classes. In my exuberant, ignorant haste I committed my Travelall to the less-experienced Windham day class. The college class was light years ahead in quality of instruction and student craftsmanship. The Windham day class was more nineteenth-century.

I found the Windham auto body teacher reclined in an inmate-made chair with his head buried in the sports section of the *Houston Chronicle*. He looked almost cartoonish, with his frail frame, patched muttonchops, and thin white hair combed over his oily, balding scalp. Maybe he was born in the nineteenth century, because he sure did look old enough, just like a caricature lifted right out of the pages of *Harper's Weekly!* I stood unnoticed for some time before he peered over the edge of his newspaper, evidently irked by my intrusion.

"*Yes*, and what can I do you for?" he grumbled.

"I've heard you can fix my dented fender."

"For prison staff, sure, but I've never seen the likes of you 'round here."

"That's because I'm new. I'm an art teacher with Windham."

"You shittin' me, boy? I've never heard of any art classes at Ferguson, and I can tell you I've been around here plenty long enough to know that!"

"No, sir, I'm shooting you straight," I fired back. "Dr. Murray personally appointed me to pilot a new program for the inmates." This seemed to get his attention. "I've been told that all prison staff can depend upon your students for good body work. My Travelall is waiting just outside, if you care to take a look."

My sights were locked on his glum mug but his eyes were shifty, avoiding contact with mine. *I don't like this guy*, I thought. *But I need his help. Guess I'll have to trust him.*

Through thin metal-rimmed bifocals, he reluctantly surveyed the damage to my Travelall. I asked him to paint it "school bus yellow" instead of green. I've always liked green cars, yet some people can't see it when driving in areas where there's thick vegetation. So I figured bright yellow would attract more attention, and hopefully prevent a repeat of the Henry and Eunice Show.

"You'll have to buy the supplies," crowed the auto body instructor, "which includes sixty pounds of Bondo. You must also pay a $2.00 fee to the vocational department office, before *any work* can begin!"

"No problem," I answered back.

I was happy to pay it, and a few days later I went to pay the two bucks to the day shift officer in charge of the vocational department. This guy was just as eerie as the auto body teacher: Very tall and thin, he looked about sixty years old but fit for his age, with a stone serious face behind brown plastic-rimmed bifocals. His voice croaked from decades of heavy smoking.

"Mr. Humphries, are you *sure* that you want the *Windham* auto body class to work on your vehicle?" How he emphasized "sure" and "Windham" bothered me.

"Well, I've already purchased the Bondo and I can't afford to go elsewhere, so why not?"

He sat down slowly behind his desk, staring at me as if pondering his next move in an invisible chess match. I had a feeling I was walking into some kind of trap.

After few days of carpooling and bus riding, I began to wonder how my Travelall was coming along. So I paid the auto shop an unannounced visit. And as usual, the Windham teacher was leaning back in his chair reading his newspaper. "How's my truck coming along?" I asked. Without looking up from his reading, he pointed to where two young African Americans were struggling with the dent. Seeing that everything was in order, though miffed by the teacher's apathy, I told him I'd check back in a week, leaving the teacher still seated at full tilt, nose buried in what appeared like the classifieds.

Unfortunately, two crucial weeks passed before I was able to visit the shop again. As I walked across the vocational area on my way to the body shop, I spotted the vocational department officer in full sprint, his long legs stretched out to intercept my path.

"Mr. Humphries! Don't go in there! I need you to come with me," he panted.

"Is there a problem?" I asked.

"Just come to the office. I need to . . . ask a favor of you."

In his office, the officer sat down behind his desk, insisting I too take a seat.

"I'd rather stand." Something was amiss.

Leaning toward me over his desk, he described the situation in a low, determined voice.

"Before you look at your vehicle, I want you to be ready to prepare me a letter describing its condition, in *full detail*. With that I can submit it with my own report to the supervisor."

Something's definitely not right.

"That damn auto body teacher should be fired, I tell you, but he's been clever enough to finagle some kind of explanation to cover up his shoddy work. Hah! Not anymore, because now, I have your truck as evidence."

This cannot be good.

His intensity set me on edge. I backed out of his office without a word and hurried to the body shop. I could not possibly imagine what the hell had happened! Nor was I surprised to find the teacher behind his desk, reading his newspaper again.

"Where's my vehicle," I demanded, trying to hide my anxiety.

"Just outside," he replied, pointing to an open garage door. Soon it became clear what an awful teacher he really was. Outside the shop sat my once-green Travelall, now painted in school bus yellow, as per my request. But so were the windows, the windshield, and even the tires, painted yellow! The students hadn't masked off anything, painting the whole damn vehicle yellow, from grille to gate!

I was in too much shock to scream. The fender was worse than before. The students did nothing about mending the six-inch deep dent. They just filled the crushed in fender with Bondo, which somehow also sealed the passenger door shut. Now my stomach twisted in agony.

My poor Travelall, what have they done to you?

Then I opened the door to look inside.

I wanted to scream but all the breath had left my body. The whole interior was yellow. Everything! The dash, gauges, rug, seats, even *the inside of the windows*! Stunned, I shut my vehicle's door and stumbled over to the body shop teacher's desk, trying to regain my composure.

"Have you checked my vehicle?" I hissed in my most conservative tone.

"Did a good job, didn't they," he smiled over his newspaper.

"Oh, yeah, they sure did," I growled back. "In fact they did such a good job, I'm going to ask the vocational supervisor to come and see what fine work your students have done to my truck!"

It took all of my will to keep my wits as I scuttled off to seal his fate. Funny thing is, as I dashed away, he actually dropped his newspaper and ran over to see my truck. I stopped at the vocational department office, glanced briefly in the direction of the auto body shop, turned to the officer and hollered, "You'll have a letter from me within the hour!" He nodded, looking completely unsurprised by my reaction.

When I got to my classroom, I paused for a moment before beginning my letter on how the auto shop totally screwed up my truck. That's when I remembered a book titled *Games People Play* by Dr. Eric Berne, about his theories of Transactional Analysis, and realized that I had become a pawn in someone else's game.

And so it was that I figured that, unbeknownst to me before that day, a game was being played between this officer and the Windham auto body teacher. The officer had been patiently waiting to spring a trap on that teacher after his shop screwed up another job. And my injured Travelall was to be the bait. Later, I figured out that he needed documented evidence of the teacher's incompetence. As luck would have it, I walked right into this twisted game I felt was created by the officer's beast.

I also later learned that it was standard operating procedure to use people in this way at TDC (Inmates called this game "Shot in the Cross,"), except here the TDC staff played it on each other. It makes you feel stupid, helpless and used. The unfortunate one caught in the crossfire is forced to side with the perpetrator of the set-up in order to extricate himself. Truly gives a new dimension to the phrase "I got set up."

My thoughts were shaken when the schoolhouse phone rang. I knew who was on the other line. A breathless, almost incoherent voice pleaded, "We'll fix it! We'll fix it! Don't worry, Mr. Humphries, all will be fixed. They'll clean it up! It'll be okay, I promise!"

"You're damn right it will be fixed," I sneered back. "*Everything* about this foul-up will be fixed!"

The situation was ludicrous. It was inconceivable to me that any teacher of any subject would allow his or her students to commit such an error without correction or discipline. Guess he was asleep at the wheel but by then I was angry and wanting justice. I banged out my letter in furious haste and personally delivered it to the vocational supervisor. He sprang from his seat as I barged into his office and tossed him my letter in disgust. Without taking the time to listen to his remarks, I bolted from the office, mad at the whole lot of them. It also made me sad that this auto body instructor was an employee of the Windham School System. All of the Windham teachers I met had been, until now, very serious and professional in doing their job. I thought of ways to retaliate but then resolved that even incompetent teachers must be allowed due process. The auto body teacher continued in his job for the duration of that year's contract, which was not renewed. Someone mentioned he had decided it was time to retire, but I figured it differently.

The paint was removed from the windows and the leatherette upholstery. Yet, it was obvious to my friends or any passerby that my Travelall was a victim of shoddy work. Ever the optimist, I found humor in how horrid it looked and christened it "The Bondo Special." The truck served me well for many months afterward, until I hit the side of a small foothill outside of Austin. Fortunately, I walked away but The Bondo Special was finished.

Away and Back Again

Charlie Lindsay and the Road to Ellis

THE BEAST PROWLS THE PSYCHE and attempts to nibble at our soul every day, and though some of us are apt at keeping it at bay, some fall victim to its relentless gnawing. As the years passed, some friends and family lost their spirit to keep on living, allowing the beast to chew up their minds and bodies until nothing remained. Such is the sad truth of what happened to my good friend Charlie.

In the spring of 1974, I decided to leave my job at the TDC to move to Austin and open my own art studio (a decision that would be reversed all too soon). By the time I left, though, Barbara Lindsay, my fellow teacher and mentor, and her husband Charlie had become close friends of mine, a friendship that started soon after I started working at Ferguson. They knew about my divorce and how I lived in an obscure part of town, so before long, I had a couple of new friends in Huntsville. They visited me every week, Charlie with a pot of his famous Cajun gumbo and Barbara with her exquisite lemon meringue pies. The two of them helped me fight back my own beast at a time when I needed another's aid most.

The two of them were polar opposites: Charlie was a retired chemical engineer and Barbara was a schoolteacher. Barbara was bright and cheerful; Charlie was bipolar and an alcoholic. As one of my colleagues at Ferguson, Barbara's positivity helped level the score between the "lions and the Christians," even when the odds ran heavily in favor of the lions.

Sometimes I would show up at the Lindsays' home for a few drinks of bourbon and water, while Charlie would stoically demonstrate his

resolve with his ever-present glass of southern iced tea. We discussed politics, religion, work and small-town living for hours. Charlie would eventually prepare a bowl of his favorite snack before going to bed: Blue Bell Homemade Vanilla ice cream and Oreo cookies. The way Charlie ate you would think he'd gain weight but he never did. His nickname was "Bones," since no matter what he ate he remained boney thin. Usually he was jovial and good-natured: This was the side of him everyone liked.

Charlie's outlook on life was simple: Do your best to do good. He referred to God as his "Ol' Higher Power," and whenever a fellow alcoholic had a problem, he was the first to go see him and work through the Twelve Steps. But when he got into one of his dark tempers, even Barbara couldn't stand to be around him. As he told me, those were the times he felt trapped in a valley of despair, overwhelmed by surges of manic depression, and his only remedy was alcohol. Regardless, he was a good husband to Barbara and a dear friend of mine.

That spring in Austin was supposed to be a good time for me. Commissions for portraits and commercial drafting quickly came my way soon after I had arrived, and for a little over three months I lived in bliss with this dream. A dream that came to an unexpected halt when a despondent Barbara phoned me with terrible news: Charlie had committed suicide using his shotgun. My shock was only stifled by Barbara's deep, despondent sobs as she garbled out a plea for my help. With a lump in my throat, I managed to say I would be there for her. I hung up and cried my eyes dry. *Damn, Charlie, was that the best you could do? How could you take the easy way out and leave Barbara alone?*

I was an adopted member of the Lindsay family now, so the death of Charlie devastated me. Barbara needed someone close at hand to talk with and help out around the house, but her children lived far away. Charlie's death made it clear I was needed back in Huntsville. The news of his death fed my own personal darkness, making it almost impossible to paint or draw or even eat. It was in that dire hour, I realized I too needed to be a part of a family who cared about me.

I suggested to Barbara's family that I return to Huntsville, stay in Barbara's guestroom, and help in any way I could in maintaining their property. They accepted my offer and in no time I packed some essentials into my blue 1971 Pontiac Grandville, and gave away anything that didn't fit into the car. It was a Texas July, and the Sunday morning sun after Mass was already sweltering. I asked the father for his blessing, hopped into my Pontiac with its faulty air conditioner, and began my trip back to Huntsville.

The next day, I phoned John Rathke, a Windham administrator, about the getting my old job back.

"Sorry, Mr. Humphries, we found an art teacher for Ferguson when you left, and Walls has halted their study on art therapy. We don't seem to need you right now."

"Well, are there *any* teacher openings?" I pressed.

"Hmm, let me see." The shuffling of papers was all I heard, then a long silence. Finally, he picked up.

"Okay, looks like we do need teacher at the Ellis Unit, but it's in math so—"

"I can do it!" I interrupted. "I'm Texas-certified to teach secondary math!"

"Well, looks like you just got hired. Can you start tomorrow?"

"Absolutely!"

The next day I met Ben Small, principal of the Windham School at the Ellis Unit. He led me along a brief tour of the prison. The Ellis Unit was essentially the same as the Ferguson Unit but with heavier industry and its own death row, where inmates were held before their executions at the main prison. Approximately two-thirds of the men were serving a life sentence for murder, but that didn't bother me one iota. I had a job, a place to stay and my old friends close by. I hadn't a care in the world to worry about, but even that was short lived.

My tenure at Ellis lasted only until the end of the summer of 1974. Just days after I was rehired the Carrasco hostage crisis began. And that changed the lives of us all.

The Beast Shows Its Face: The Carrasco Hostage Crisis

On July 23, 1974, I was eating lunch with Father Joseph O'Brien, Ellis's prison chaplain, in the officers' dining hall at Ellis, when a telephone call came for him. Without another word, he left immediately. I later learned that he had gone to the Walls Unit and volunteered to join a group of Windham District teachers who had been taken hostage that day by the notorious heroin kingpin of South Texas, Fred Gomez Carrasco.

Soon after I had returned to my class, I noticed something was amiss. None of my students had returned from chow. Instead, all inmates had been ordered to their cells until further notice. I wandered down the hallway and soon found the other teachers huddled around a security officer. They all looked worried, so I joined their group to find out what was happening.

"What's the matter?" I asked the officer.

"There is a situation at the Walls Unit right now," he responded, "and all non-security personnel are required to go home immediately. That is all I can tell you."

I took the hint and left for my home moments later. In the military, when orders are given where any subsequent information is provided on a "need-to-know" basis, you high tail it to your post and don't ask any questions. But as soon as I turned on the radio, my suspicions were confirmed. Some inmates at Walls were trying to escape, and had taken Windham teachers as hostages. I couldn't help but think, *"That could've been me!"*

As told by Dr. Ronald Robinson, one of the surviving hostages, in his book *Prison Hostage: The Siege of the Walls Prison in Huntsville, Texas*, on July 23, 1974, Carrasco and three other inmates, armed with three .357 magnum revolvers and 150 bullets, took control of the Huntsville Unit law library. This turned into the longest hostage crisis in American penal history, until the fifteen-day stand off that took place at Arizona's Louis Prison in 2004.

For the next eleven days, FBI agents and the Texas Rangers negotiated for the release of the hostages. On the eleventh day, the convicts attempted to escape. They constructed what some reporters called the "Trojan Taco"—a makeshift shield of mobile chalkboards further shielded by thick law books for bulletproofing—in an attempt to wheel down the ramp from the schoolhouse to a waiting armored car in the prison yard, which would they hoped would take them to the airport where they would board a flight to Cuba. Carrasco and the others also took along four hostages as human shields inside the Taco.

The Texas Rangers dashed Carrasco's plans to flee to Cuba by breaking through the Trojan Taco's fortified walls with a high-pressured fire hose. In the following chaos, gunfire erupted as the Texas Rangers rushed up the ramp. Carrasco and fellow conspirator Rodolfo Dominguez murdered hostages Julia Standley, a librarian, and special education teacher Von Beseda during the mêlée. Both convicts died at the scene.

Father O'Brien, who was also used as a human shield, suffered a chest wound but, luckily, survived. Ignacio Cuevas, a third inmate conspirator, was captured and later executed by lethal injection in 1991. Other hostage survivors included Dr. Robinson, who was a teacher; Jack Branch; Bertha Davis; Principal Novella Pollard; education consultant Glenn Johnson; librarians Aline House, Linda Woodman, and Ann Fleming; and correctional officer Bobby Heard.

As the investigation of the siege continued, word went out that Windham teachers were needed to replace the previous staff at the Walls Unit. I volunteered to teach math there until a replacement could be found. Soon, I would be continuing the art program started by Golda Rich after I left Walls the first time. Due to a harrowing part she'd played in the Carrasco siege, she decided it would be best to take some time off.

As I learned later, Ignacio Cuevas, the third inmate conspirator, had been one of her art students. Minutes before the takeover, he asked to see her privately. Golda took him to one side and asked what the fuss was about, but Ignacio just kept insisting she leave the school immediately. As TDC staff, we all developed internal radars for trouble, so when a good student warns you of imminent danger, you do what he says. As she safely walked to her car outside the red brick walls of the Walls Unit, she heard the news that teachers were being attacked and held hostage.

Golda left just moments before Carrasco, Cuevas, and Dominguez brandished their revolvers and took most of the school's staff into the library, where they held out for the next eleven days. It was our worst nightmare: being held against your will at gunpoint by men who had little to lose.

Later, after it was over, I caught up with Golda as she was leaving Walls. Golda had put in many years of service at Windham, years that had honed her senses against inmate trouble. She remarked to me how she didn't hesitate to question why Ignacio had been so insistent and so nervous.

"It was how he looked at me, Jim," she recalled. "You don't doubt a man who looks at you with eyes of a beast."

"What do you mean by that, Golda?" The tone of her voice gave me an eerie feeling.

"He had this blank look, as if something else had taken over him and swallowed his soul. He looked straight through me, Jim. Straight through the depths of my soul!" I could see her tremble. "My preacher told me only Beelzebub, *The Beast*, can make a man look like that, behave like that."

"Like he was possessed?"

"Uh-huh! Oh honey, I hope you never have to see what I saw! You won't forget it, because bad things always follow a man with that sort of look. Now let's stop all this talk, okay Jim? It has caused me to lose too many nights of sleep already!"

Strange how her words rang in my head: *Something else had taken him over and swallowed his soul.* The way I looked at it, the beast had occupied his body, eating away at his humanity, only to use him as a vessel for murder without mercy.

I became so lost in my thoughts about what had happened, I drove right past my home without stopping and found myself pulling into the church parking lot. *Yes, Jim, I think this is just the place to sort all this out.*

Huntsville: Reconstruction

For a while after the Carrasco siege, all activities in the Walls Unit prison yard were cancelled. Gone were the sounds of inmate life. Gone were the clanking of metal weights and the exuberant domino games the inmates enjoyed so much. All that remained was a dead silence. The schoolhouse had been one of the only places where an inmate could be a student and not a convict. But our sanctuary had been desecrated, our teachers murdered.

Finally, after weeks of rotating our classes amongst the few spare rooms inside the other cellblocks, the uneasy silence was broken during that morning's roll call. The banging hammers, buzzing saws, and whizzing drills of the TDC Construction Department came as a relief to everyone, for the rebuilding of the school and library had begun.

Inside the school's entrance was a maintenance closet with a large electric circuit breaker. I remember the metal border of this box because of the single bullet hole that still remained in it. It was a grim reminder of prison violence. The beast had devoured two of our own and planted a painful memory in the survivors, their friends and family, and anyone closely associated with those eleven days in July.

For a few weeks, employees and inmates alike were uncomfortable about returning to the school. But, under the leadership of our new principal Chris Tracy, we all settled into getting our schoolhouse back to as close to normal as possible. Soon enough, I continued my work with patients in the treatment center, and slowly, life returned to normal.

Sweetheart from Venezuela

Though my professional life was shrouded in uncertainty after the hostage crisis, I did find joy outside of work. She was a beautiful South American girl who sang in the church choir I had joined after Charlie's death. During that autumn in 1974, I tried my earnest to talk with her but it was no use. She didn't seem to like me much and always was being whisked away by her friends right after choir practice. So, I settled for telling her nice things during break as she passed by, which usually resulted in her looking at me with a strange frown. But I didn't care.

Celeste was nothing like any girl I had ever seen. She walked around in miniskirts and knee-high boots while all the other girls were covered up in long skirts and wore platform shoes. She wore colorful make-up and bright colors at a time when the more simple, natural look was popular. And as much as I tried to get to know her, the more she eluded me. Finally, by the spring of 1975, things had changed. Celeste gave me hope that true love does happen to men like me.

My first wife knew I wanted to start a family before we were married but she failed to mention that she couldn't have children, having waited until our wedding day to inform me of this peculiar detail. We had met quite young and dated through college. I turned down a full tuition art scholarship to the University of Pennsylvania, so I could stay in Jackson, Mississippi, and go to the same private college she attended. We were both artists who were in love with each other's talent, but it wasn't until we got married that I saw a different side of her.

She had no sympathy for my military background or sense of patriotism. One afternoon, I came home from my job at Boeing to find she had thrown my Marine Corps dress uniform in the trash basket. She told me she didn't think I needed it anymore and that I should throw it away. We had been growing apart for some time by then, so I figured if I made a sacrifice like this, she would appreciate me more. But that walk to the dumpster was one of the longest walks of my life. Putting my uniform into the trash felt terrible, just terrible.

I tried to walk back inside but I just couldn't. *"This isn't right, Jim,"* I thought. *"You can't let someone take away your memories."* So,

I decided to keep only my formal hat, and to this day it sits safely in my closet. Not surprisingly, just like the rest of my uniform, that marriage went to the dump after eleven years of trying to make it work.

By the spring of 1975, I was engaged again, but not to Celeste. My fiancée was a Guatemalan gal who was simply unable to admit to me that she was using me to make another man jealous, while all along having no intention on marrying me. So she made up an elaborate lie of how Celeste, this sweet Venezuelan girl from the chorus, insisted that they both go on a church retreat on the same weekend I was to announce our engagement to my mother. I was too hurt to return to choir practice and see Celeste, the woman I thought responsible for fouling up my engagement. So I stopped attending. Then one evening, after my engagement ended, I received a phone call.

"Jim," said a thick, accented woman's voice. It was Celeste! "I no see you in church. Are you okay?"

"Everything is under control," I answered in my usual guarded tone.

"*No te creo*, Jim. You no sound good."

"Well, you are right about that. I haven't felt good about myself for some time."

"You come to church and we talk, okay?" Though I could barely make out the words through her accent, I could feel that she felt bad about something. It also felt good that someone was thinking about me, so I obliged her and attended the next choir practice.

When I saw her again, she seemed happy I was back singing. I was even more elated after she accepted my offer to drive her to choir rehearsals. Since she was new to the United States, her overly protective sponsor family thwarted every opportunity for me to get together with Celeste off campus. Likewise, getting any free time with her while she was on campus was just as impossible. Study groups and language club meetings kept her one step ahead of me. The open road was my only ally, for it was in those short drives to and from church that our relationship began.

One Sunday, she invited me over to see her new stereo. I remember how she was so proud of it, with its state-of-the-art turntable/cassette/tuner combo. She explained all the components, showed me the new records she had purchased. I tried to look interested but it was hard to concentrate as I sat on her bed, in that a tiny dorm room, with such a beautiful woman.

The day finally came when I took a leap of faith and invited her out for ice cream. Everything went just like a date should have, that is until my Pontiac decided to stall in the middle of a busy avenue. How embarrassing! Somehow though, I kept my cool and managed to get it running again. Unfortunately, I ruined my trousers and reeked of motor oil. I thought the date was over, but none of this bothered her. She was a really sweet girl.

We went back to her dorm building and sat in the parking lot until very late, just talking. That's when she made some observations about me that were very true. As she put it, "I do not like how you laugh so loud, Jim. Your jokes cannot hide the sadness in your heart." It was like she had read the chapters I'd omitted from the story of my life. It floored me that she could read me so well.

The next morning I surprised her with a present. It was the soundtrack to the movie *Jonathan Livingston Seagull* by Neil Diamond. I was helplessly smitten and as luck would have it, so was she. My life continued to move forward after we began courting, and that record, which sits on a shelf next to that same stereo today, would become the theme for our marriage.

Not everything about our courtship was peaches and cream. It was a hard sell telling both our mothers that we wanted to get married. My mother always wanted me to settle down with a good Southern girl but never expected me to fall for a South American beauty. And Celeste's mother had no interest in her daughter marrying a *gringo* seventeen years her senior, but, eventually, they both conceded that our love was true and gave us their blessing. We were married on December 21st, 1975. Not long after, on October 4th, 1976, our first son, James, was born.

It's been twenty-five wonderful years since that fateful phone call. We've lived in three cities and raised four kids, and all I can say is thank you to all my children and my beautiful wife.

Old Sparky

Back in August of 1975, I was relieved from my job as a math teacher, and was assigned to resurrecting the art program. I was also asked to help with the Inmate Rodeo Art Show, a tradition held every Sunday in October, in conjunction with the annual Huntsville Prison Rodeo. Soon I was involved with the Inmate Fine Arts Festival, directing the preparations of artwork for this event. That year we were forced to use the death row cellblock because of the extra room it provided due to the federal moratorium on capital punishment. Each state was ordered to reexamine its capital punishment laws and procedures in an effort to ensure that every execution would not be considered cruel and unusual punishment.

Our new E&R officer, whom I'll call Mr. Hallinan, required all the teachers and staff to attend his tour of the Walls Unit death row and execution chamber as part of the orientation for new faculty. We were shown the inmate holding cells, the area for the witnesses, and Old Sparky, the infamous Texas electric chair. Finally, the director insisted on demonstrating every detail of an execution by electrocution.

Old Sparky was a rigid, ninety-degree angle oak chair that definitely was not designed for comfort. The condemned inmate was forced to sit upright, with leather restraint straps secured across his arms, legs and chest.

"Now these here are called *ee-leck-trodes*," Mr. Hallinan emphasized. "They're attached to each leg and arm. Then we take a sponge, soak it in saltwater and place it on the head. It's *very* important this gets done, cuz the head will cook and smell this place up to high heavens! Oooowee! Let me tell you there ain't nothin' more rank than a human head on fire!"

Just the thought of burning human flesh turned just about everyone's stomach, something he seemed to delight in.

"Hey! Don't y'all lose your lunch on me now! I haven't even gotten to the good stuff."

Why *did* we have this tour after another day of mystery meat? I wondered. It was a cruel thing to force us teachers to hear about this stuff after lunch, especially from such an unusually enthusiastic guide.

"Before we get the *condemned* into the chair," he went on, "we shave a spot on his head, right here."

He bent over and drew a small circle around his own bald spot.

"The head must be shaved to insure *po-si-tive eee-leck-tri-kal con-tact*. We then take this here bit, and put it in the mouth. And then, we cover his face with this." Like a magician pulling a rabbit from a hat, he proudly produced a leather mask from the bag he had been carrying.

"Y'all probably thinking, why do we need a mask?" He paused and flashed us a sly smile. "Well, it keeps the brain, eyes, and other bodily fluids from, well, alarming the witnesses. Hell, I've heard stories about the times before we used masks. The head would literally explode, all over those sitting in the room!"

I turned away and winced, tasting the mystery meat rising at the back of my throat. He seemed pleased by my reaction and paused to let the awful visuals simmer in our minds. But after we had thwarted his attempt to make us ill, he shrugged and led us to the room behind the electric chair.

"Here we control the flow of electricity. The inmate receives two surges, to insure complete death. Remember the floor where the witnesses sat, in front of the chair? It's covered with a rubber mat. We've figured electricity can be unpredictable, so it's only a precautionary measure to ensure we only have one dead man when it's all over. And that concludes your orientation. Y'all have a nice day now!"

As it turned out, that wouldn't be the last time I would be in the same room with that chair. Since the schoolhouse was under construction, the only place with extra space where we could mat artwork was the death row block. I couldn't bear to be in that place for too long, so I let the inmates figure out how to work with it.

When I visited them the following school day, I found that they had brought in worktables. But they were also using Old Sparky to prop up the largest works. I ordered them to immediately remove our artwork from that throne of death, then had the chair crated up and removed from our work area. It never ceased to amaze me how nonchalant the inmates' attitude toward death was. I wouldn't go near that thing, but they simply picked it up and moved it just like any another piece of furniture.

Finally, news came from the warden that Old Sparky was headed for the Smithsonian Museum in Washington, D.C. Before then, however, it was crated back up and returned to our work area, despite my protests. At that point, I decided to make the best of the situation and use it as a surface mat for artwork. Just being in that holding room for condemned men reaffirmed my belief that anyone who works in a prison must develop their own personal defense system, for the mere sake of their sanity. The Walls Unit death house reverberated with old, ugly vibrations, but we had a job to do and it needed doing. As it turned out, this would be the last time anyone would ever perform outside work within the execution area, for it had been earmarked for remodeling to accommodate a new form of execution: death by lethal injection.

Mr. Orange Peels

As I was resurrecting the art program at the Walls, many of the established inmate artists would visit me and introduce themselves. These men worked in a variety of prison jobs: laundry, air conditioning, auto repair, building maintenance, and printing. I was not surprised to find that most of them worked for the printing department because of the creative outlet it gave them.

I commissioned one such artist, Curtis, to create an album cover for a client in the free world. Curtis possessed an excellent sense of design, so I only acted as an advisor. I asked him if he ever had any formal art training, a question that brought a yelp of laughter.

"Boss, my family never saw a need for art," Curtis drawled.

"But you *had* to have had *some* kind of training to draft designs like these," I insisted.

"Well, let me just say that when I draw, it kinda calms me down," he continued. "I've got to have clean lines in my art 'cause it makes me relax when I look at it. Suppose it's the only two blessings God gave me: steady hands and good eyes."

I had been around many graphic designers, but the natural talent Curtis displayed rivaled the skills of designers who'd been educated at some of the best design schools in the nation.

His genial personality only complimented his uncanny design work. Ever the opportunist, he told me he refused to work in the printing department many times because his job with the air conditioning section of building maintenance served him well. He summed up his reason in one sentence: "Everyone likes to be comfortable, boss. Even the Warden." Not long after, I learned what he meant by his puzzling answer.

East Texas is damned hot nearly all year long, and prison life can wear down anyone's patience if you're sweating all day. As a reputable A/C repair inmate with a good sense of humor, Curtis was the favorite among the prison department heads, especially Major Murdock. Occasionally though he would find himself confronted by the Major and have to explain another one of his creative endeavors—such as his orange peel ceiling.

The inmate artists at Walls desired any environment that inspired their muse. When possible, most of them requested to be moved to the upper run of East Wing. Built circa 1848, this section had a Wild West kind of atmosphere. The wooden floor and ceiling of decorative sheet metal stamped in relief, lent a different feeling to this area. I too enjoyed my walks among these cells, for the cold steel and concrete of the lower levels robbed the creative mind of peace. You didn't have to be an inmate to lose a bit of your tranquility when among these walls. I felt that the more I spent working among the clanking doors and clunking locks below, the less I would want to paint, draw and express the gifts that God had given me.

Not long after Curtis moved into his cell on the upper run, I happened to be walking in the neighborhood, sorting through my thoughts, when Major Murdock paid Curtis a visit. As the Major inspected the cell, he noted the smell of fresh oranges. One look up solved the mystery: Orange peels had been taped all over the ceiling, everywhere!

"What is that!" barked Major Murdock as he pointed upward.

With his usual dose of jolly, Curtis smiled and proudly announced, "Room deodorizer, sir!"

Major Murdock glared, shook his head, and then his expression softened. He pushed his hat back on his head and walked off, grinning to himself. No mention of the incident came up again. Later, over plates of mystery meat, I asked the Major why he said nothing to the inmate about the orange peels.

"He's the best A/C tech we got, so I figure he can enjoy a decent smelling cell for all the good work he's done over the years."

Often the inmates would find themselves preoccupied by the circumstances that had brought them to prison. Mr. Orange Peels was no exception. Sometimes his wonderful, though frequently bizarre, sense of humor would fail him. Then his voice would strain and choke as he recalled how he had wound up in prison. He'd started out as an heir to the fortune of a prominent Texas family. After inheriting that large sum of money, he went on a yearlong spending spree that finished with him financially broke and deep in a heroin addiction.

Then he met a parolee versed in the ways of armed robbery. Desperate to feed his beast's hunger for heroin, Curtis took to robbing liquor stores. One day he accidentally dropped his wallet at the scene of an otherwise successful robbery. Soon thereafter, he was arrested and sentenced to ten years. His family hired a good lawyer and he was paroled within two years, but he left the state without permission and was remanded back to prison with a "serve all" stipulation. He remained a little over seven years before completing his sentence, which was reduced only by his good behavior.

Curtis told me he was considered the black sheep of the family. I know this weighed heavily on his mind, for at times during class his usual smile was replaced with the sort of blank eyes Golda Rich had described. I took to counseling him, determined not to let the beast within him win another man's soul. It was during those dark moments I'd casually ask him what troubled thoughts stole away his smile.

"Why did you turn to armed robbery for money?"

"Power," he said, staring off with a haunting look. "You can't imagine the sense of power I had when I pointed a gun in someone's face and told them to give me their money."

"Well, you have a much greater power, and it doesn't take a gun to make it happen. Now why don't you show me what you've been working on?"

These nonchalant suggestions usually pulled Curtis back to reality. His eyes would fill with tears that he quickly wiped away. The smile would return to his face, and then he would produce a fine example of the day's assignment.

Curtis's odd sense of humor often covered up the deep, self-inflicted wounds to his soul, wounds that could not heal because he felt that his family would never forgive him. Though he had not spoken to any of them since his incarceration, he assumed the worst. While the State of Texas had sentenced his body to custody, Curtis tortured his own soul every day. This specter of guilt haunted him, as it haunted numerous other inmates, robbing each one of them of any peace.

After completing his TDC sentence, he moved as far as possible into the Big Thicket forest of East Texas, far away from his former Houston criminal contacts. I lost touch with him, until years later while I was visiting the local butcher shop for some tri-tip.

That day I saw the butcher hamming it up with a neighboring bakery owner, while admiring the baker's brochure. The baker said he had it designed by a fellow who also worked magic with his bakery's

A/C. I asked to see the brochure and, sure enough, I recognized the clean lines and uncluttered style. It had to be the work of Mr. Orange Peels.

Shot in the Cross

One Friday evening as I was leaving for the weekend, I crossed paths with an inmate artist heading off to night class. Passing me with a wry smile, he said to me, "Have a good weekend! Oh, and don't you worry about what Major Murdock said about your art program!" Without giving me the chance to respond, he dashed up the school ramp.

Because I was still inexperienced with con games, I spent most of the weekend worrying about what he was referring to. Had I had known this was yet another play, with me acting my part perfectly for the inmates' amusement, I would have never let it bother me. The guards were privy to the inmates' underhanded schemes, but Windham staff paled in experience and thus suffered the humiliation.

First thing Monday morning, I was at Major Murdock's office. With tired eyes, I relayed what had been told to me. When I reached the part where I said, "an inmate told me," he cut short my story and dismissed the inmate bookkeepers sitting nearby. He ordered me to take a seat. Sitting with his back fully erect, the Major crossed his arms and scowled: "Mr. Humphries, if I want you to know something I'll tell you myself directly, not relay it through an inmate!"

"Sir, I was unaware—" but he again interrupted me, insulted at my attempt to explain.

"Look here and listen up! These men will do *anything* to mess with your head. If they can upset prison staff with some fish story, it will make them ever more brazen to try some other ploy to confuse the hell out of us. I can't be babysitting Windham staff with every little complaint, so do us both a favor and leave the con games to the inmates."

With that, he sat back into his leather chair, uncrossed his arms, smirking with his eyes. "Jim, you just got shot in the cross! Sorry son, but I'm too old to fall for that trick."

"Shot in the *what*?"

"Shot in the cross. It's a mind game inmates play to pit two people against each other by using an unsuspecting third player. That inmate wanted you to worry yourself sick, and by the look on your face, I'd reckon he did a pretty good job of it!"

He was right. I hadn't slept a wink since Friday night and the stress had killed my appetite, too. How could I have been so careless as to forget prison protocol? Humbled, I apologized and excused myself.

"Mr. Humphries," the Major barked as I turned away. "Let me ask you something."

Whatever his question was, I hoped it would be good. My head was throbbing from the stress. "Word has it you were with the Marines?"

"Absolutely, sir."

"Yeah, I can tell by how you can take a tongue lashing, you must be Marine material," he chuckled. "I was in the Air Force myself! Hell, let me make some amends by getting you a cup of coffee. Come on in here and relax. The inmates aren't going anywhere. Plus, you could use some downtime, as I reckon you haven't gotten much shut-eye in the last three days."

For the next couple of hours, we swapped military stories over several cups of coffee, not caring about the time. The Major was a firm yet hearty man, rarely smiling and always frowning, so I felt privileged to see the humorous side of him.

After that, anytime an inmate told me something the Major supposedly had done or said, I would look the convict square in the eye and sneer back, "*Oh, really?*"

Coffee Break

One afternoon, I stopped at the dining hall for a cup of coffee. One of the officers joined me at my table, and, without warning, he started telling me all about his failures in life. Prison life can wear down all who work there, and the guards were no exception. They have to deal with the most stressful part of the job, so I sympathized whenever they talked about how rough their lives could be.

After going on for a good ten minutes, the officer looked up from his coffee with the saddest expression. "But if I just had the advantages you young folk have today, oh man, I could have done better! Everything would've been easier!"

"How old are you?" I asked.

"Thirty-six."

I did not have the heart to tell him that I was thirty-eight.

Pyramid of Food

Life as a security guard at Walls didn't appear to be physically demanding, given the size of some of the guards. Their eating habits seemed to reflect an extreme lack of concern regarding fat and cholesterol intake. One officer named Larry was especially amazing. His rotund belly reminded me of Porky Pig's, and, sadly, seeing the way he ate, you'd be tempted to think he was part pig.

Every day at chow, Larry would build himself a pyramid of mixed food servings on his plate. Layers of buttered mashed potatoes glued together at least two prime cut steaks, all intermixed with vegetables, and always accompanied by a separate mound of pudding. I'd only seen those kinds of food pyramids while I was a Marine and only during a heavy downpour during field training. Because of how the mess line was set up, the mess men were unable to see where they were placing the food on your mess kit, so the standard protocol was to "heap it up in the middle." It made otherwise bland military cooking edible, but the cooking at Walls was better: There was no reason to ruin a good steak and potatoes. For this one guard though, it was intentional, and he seemed very content as he built up and mowed down his food pyramids.

Since few officers showed up for supper, I could usually steal away after work and enjoy a peaceful meal. That was when I would

see this tremendously overweight man sitting alone with his pyramid, rapidly dispatching his dinner. Larry's method was crude yet simple: place food pyramid in direct front, lower jaw, and furiously shovel food into hovering mouth until all was gone. Repeat process for dessert pile.

He never went back for seconds because he didn't have to: He had prelayered second helpings into his first creation. Eating with incredible speed, he always finished his entire meal in less time than it took me to eat one-fourth of mine. I often wondered if he even enjoyed eating or if it was a nervous coping mechanism.

Whatever the case, it seemed right at the time. Then four years passed and the day came when I could barely recognize him. Not because he had grown to even more gargantuan proportions. No, it was the opposite: He had become gaunt and sickly. Amazed, I watched him nibble at miniscule portions of food with a languid pace, taking sips of water between tiny bites. Gone was his "open-trough, shovel-in-food" method. He sat listlessly, picking away at little morsels of cold steak and green beans. I asked an inmate cook about this drastic change in Larry's eating habits. The cook happily obliged.

"Docs called it *dye-ah-bee-tees*. Said if he don't change how he eats, he gonna die. Now all he eats is real healthy like."

"Diabetes, huh?"

"Yes sir. He told me the docs said for him to control hisself. All I said to him this whole time is he needed to quit being a damn glutton, but he paid me no mind. 'Just pile it on, boy,' is all he'd say to me. Now look at 'em, sitting there, all sad."

"I suppose," I replied, "though I never thought he looked happy the other way."

"Don't pay him no worry, boss," replied the chef. "He's lucky, you know. That stomach was gonna kill him one day."

Hog for Sale

"Sir, would you please help me?" an inmate artist named Jeff asked me one day. "I am trying to do a painting for my granddaughter." Not only was he much older than the other inmates, he was my first senior student, and since it appeared to be a noble gesture, I obliged him.

"I want to paint Jesus so my granddaughter can know that I was a good man." He handed me a small prayer card from the prison chapel as his reference.

"Sure," I replied. We sat at a desk and I began my demonstration. The idea was to help a student over a rough spot, showing them how to mix color or interpret light from a photograph. Then I'd stop and hand them the brush, pencil, or pastel, and ask them to continue what I had started. However, I would sometimes get caught up in the moment and finish it for them, and this time was no exception.

Over the next several classes, Jeff would excitedly show me his progress on the painting. Though I was perhaps too immersed in working with my other students, I did notice that the little progress he made without me was not actually progress at all. All he would do was fudge up a part I had already drawn or filled in with color, then later ask me to correct the mistake. By the final session, I couldn't resist the temptation to demonstrate how to put the finishing touches to his work. It took me two hours of my own time but it was beautiful. *"His granddaughter will definitely love this,"* I thought.

Then, a month later at the Texas Prison Rodeo, I was supervising the selling of inmate artwork. Any money an inmate received from his art was deposited in their Inmate Trust Fund account, where they could use the money to buy cigarettes and such. I was familiar with most of the work being sold, since the art was from my past or present students. But, suddenly, I saw a crowd gathering around one particular painting. I got curious and hurried over to see what was causing the commotion.

There, hanging on the metal clothesline between a crude picture of a longhorn and a landscape sketch, was the painting I had finished for my student Jeff's granddaughter! I waded through the small crowd for a closer look, not believing my eyes. Yes, it was my painting all right! And before I could gather my wits, someone had taken off the price, and replaced it with a sold tag. People clamored and protested, demanding we auction the piece. I swallowed my pride and told them the price is fixed, and when it is sold, it is sold. It hurt me to whore out a work by my own hand, because for a painting like that, I could have charged a normal, free-world client two hundred dollars. But there my work hung, in its modest paper frame, sold for just twenty bucks.

The whole day was a blur after that. My head was swimming. I couldn't decide to be sad or mad but whatever the case, I was going to let that inmate have it the next time I saw him in class. Unfortunately, that day never happened. By the next Monday morning, his name was off my roster, by his own request. Luckily, I had made friends with one of the guards, who took me to his cell later that day. The old man was lazily sitting on his bunk, munching on a Snickers bar, twirling an unopened pack of menthols.

"Hey, I saw our painting at the rodeo! You told me that was for your granddaughter, so she could remember you as a good man! How could you do that?"

He chewed on a bit of caramel in silence, looking nonchalantly at the ceiling. Finally, he just shrugged.

"I don't have a granddaughter, and even if I did, why would I tell you?" he scoffed, annoyed by my intrusion. "Now would you mind? I'm trying to enjoy my candy bar. It's been ages since I had any money to buy one."

With that he leaned back into his bunk, munching and twirling, staring at nothing. The whole situation incensed me to the core, but I couldn't let my emotions get the best of me. I stormed out of his cell, passing the smirking guard who had heard it all. "Looks like you bought his hog," snickered the guard. I was far too upset to respond because I knew this incident would quickly wind its way through the gossip grapevine.

In prison talk, when you "buy a man's hog," you're being hoodwinked into believing an elaborate lie. Jeff had fabricated a story about painting a picture of Jesus for his granddaughter, and then fed this slop to his gullible art teacher, all so he could enjoy some candy and smokes. Once again, I had been played for a fool.

And so the score stood: Inmates 2, Humphries 0.

Playboys and Pastels

Sam had lost most of his fingers. As he told it, a local drug dealer cut one of them off for every bad debt he couldn't pay. Not wanting to lose all his digits, Sam ran down the dealer with his truck. Now he was serving a twenty-year sentence for murder.

His was a typical story you'd hear in prison and didn't interest me at all. But I was intrigued by his desire to learn drawing, since I never taught a disabled artist before. We worked closely together through many classes in the hope that he'd find a way to hold the pencil with his stubs. When completed, both my student's name and mine were written on every collaborative work. Much to my chagrin, I later found he was erasing my name from our drawings and trading them for cigarettes. After discovering this, I ceased allowing any student to take my drawings out of class.

Another con game was to ask for help with a drawing of a loved one, but I had enough of this con after the Jesus-painting incident. Apparently, my class drawings also met a similar fate. They'd become a hot commodity between the inmates, where one sketch could be bartered for a pack of cigarettes or, even worse, adult magazines!

Occasionally though, I did draw demonstration portraits in class. They were only quick, fifteen-minute impressionistic charcoal sketches, or thirty-minute pastel portraits using a limited palette. The problem was that the inmate's reward for posing was that he could keep my sketch. All it took was two weeks until I received a complaint, not from the school, but from an established inmate artist at Walls. He griped to my principal that I was interfering with his inmate portrait business, since his customers could get a better one, free of charge, in my class. So, I just stopped giving inmates any of my art at Walls, and life went on.

Every once and a while, I would see my old sketches in cells of prisoners who never attended art class. I remember a particularly proud owner of one of my pastels. He told me it was his favorite possession while he was in prison, and seeing that simple picture taped to his wall made him feel more at home. It did make me feel good to hear that, and even better when he told me what he traded for it.

"I gave all my best *Playboys* for that picture, and I wouldn't give it up for all the smut in the world!"

An Unlikely Forger

If you met Chad, you would never believe he had committed felony forgery.

One day, Principal Tracy called me in to his office and offered me a cup of coffee. He only made such an offer when his visitor needed to stay a while. I was still groggy from another sleepless night, courtesy of my baby son James, so I happily took a cup.

"Jim, we have an inmate in our school who is causing quite a stir," began the principal. "He is demanding we accept him into one of our vocational programs for drafting and design."

"Okay, so what's wrong with that? If he can't draw, we can train him," I answered.

"And train him we will, but there is one problem: He doesn't have hands."

"Really?" I choked on my coffee in disbelief, spitting a little on the principal's desk. I always carried a paper towel in my back pocket for unforeseen coffee expectorations. This I quickly deployed to wipe up the mess. Thankfully, the principal was more amused than repulsed. After I regained my composure, he continued.

"Now, this inmate could get special vocational training, but only if he can prove that he's been trained in commercial sign layout."

"I see," I answered. Puzzled as to why I was being told all this, I asked, "Don't we have design and drafting teachers who can evaluate his claim?"

"Yes, we have design teachers. But I also took a quick look at the résumés we have on file and yours shows ten years of commercial art and illustration experience. And you have quite the reputation around here for connecting with the inmates, so I want you to investigate this for me."

"Thank you, sir, but I'm a little surprised you chose me for this." I sighed and thought for a second. "Oh, what the hell, it will be a good change of pace to do some drafting."

I left his office walking a bit taller than usual, happy to know my hard work had not gone unnoticed. That afternoon I drew up an adequate test to determine if this inmate had the skills and knowledge of a sign layout artist. He would need to use all the tools of the trade: drawing board, paper, pencil, eraser, ruler, and a T-square.

The next class day, I sent for Chad, the handless forger. In no time he began working, using his toes to grasp the pencils as delicately as my fingers. He shifted the drawing board around on the floor with his feet and drew perfect lines with the T-square. Before I could check on him, he was done, passing with a perfect score.

"In all my years in art," I exclaimed, "I have never met anyone like you! How do you do it?"

"Well sir, I don't know what it would be like to have arms," he replied. "I was born this way, so my feet are my hands."

News of his talent raced through Windham, and people were talking. A week later, I received word that many V.I.P.'s were coming

to see him draw. When that day arrived, a crowd filled the conference room, with film crews and photographers vying for a good vantage point. From Superintendent Dr. Murray to the Huntsville Unit warden and school principal, from local newspaper reporters to Houston's News Channel 11, they were all clamoring with excitement to see the drafting talents of Chad, the handless inmate.

As we walked into the classroom, the room hushed. Chad sat down and looked up at the people, his eyes wide from all the attention. I taped an 18 × 24 inch sheet of white paper to a drawing board and placed it on the floor in front of him along with the same implements as before. I noticed the floor was not the hard linoleum but red plush carpet, which would make this even more interesting. It didn't bother him one bit, for he only whispered me one question.

"What should I draw?" he muttered anxiously.

"Your name," I replied, "but in Gothic letters."

I stepped back and watched him go to town. As he went about his work, only the sound of clicking cameras and murmurs were audible. This was my first time seeing him create a drawing and it was nothing short of amazing. He used his feet as deftly as any artist used their hands. The finished product was precise and clean, without a single mistaken line.

The crowd of prison staff and reporters gushed with exuberant praise, all wanting to have their pictures taken with Chad. Afterward, as we walked back to his cell, I noticed tears streaming down his cheeks. I placed my arm over his shoulder and assured him he was a good man and a fine artist. He shuffled back into his cell, his head hung low, but before I left he looked up and smiled. I knew that smile when I saw it: For on that day, he felt like a man who mattered in the world.

An Unusual Perspective

Before he came to Walls, Carl had been a truck driver. At the time he joined my class, he was the head inmate gardener, tending to all the plants in the prison courtyard. Standing at about six feet two, two hundred and twenty pounds, with broad shoulders and short blonde hair, he loomed over most of the inmates. Yet, he spoke in a soft, gentle whisper.

His eagerness to learn drawing was obvious from the moment I met him. I started him out with my linear design exercises. He was a quick study and soon progressed on to linear perspective. Then his mind gave off a creative spark.

"Mr. Humphries," he asked, "how do I create a road going off in the distance, like it's going over hills and not flat land? You know how you drive over roads that seem to go on straight forever but they go over hills?"

I demonstrated how to graphically visualize the hills as transparent, making it possible to visualize the change in perspective of a road coming down the far side of a hill but still hidden from the viewer. The concepts of one-, two- and three-point linear perspective, plus optical properties of color, had begun to consume him.

For the many months Carl was in my class, he never talked about himself. Day after day he came to class eager to continue his experiments into perspective and optical design with color. Soon he was using surrealistic compositions based on perspective distortions, and using flat shapes of colors juxtaposed in such a way as to create a third color by optical illusion.

I enjoyed hearing him say, "Hey, Mr. Humphries, I found a new combination I want you to see!"

He had his beast well under control, for I never saw it surface during the five years I taught at Walls.

Final Insult

One day, I arrived to find a new student standing at my classroom door, beaming with an impish grin.

"I'm the new student," Antonio announced to the class, "come to teach y'all a thing or two about art! Hey, Teach, where can you new best student sit?"

"In the back," I snapped, "with all the other beginners!"

Antonio was a Latino man of medium height in his mid-thirties who appeared friendly; in fact, he was a little *too* friendly. His eyes glittered as if he knew something no one else knew. But I forgot all about that as soon as I took notice of his artistic talents. He required very little help with his art, showing a knack for pastel, paint, or penciled works. As I moved about my students, inspecting and critiquing their work, I usually asked him if he needed any help, for which he always refused. Drawing or mixing oil color did not present a problem for him. Behind a canvas or a drawing board, he had all the faculties of a good artist. Apparently, his only real problem was with the rest of humanity.

I soon noticed that he had no friends, and how he frequently blurted out random insults at the other students, in a futile attempt to provoke a reaction. The inmates knew they had to behave themselves in the schoolhouse, because any physical or verbal outburst was a quick ticket to three days in solitary confinement, not to mention a suspension of their school privileges. They had a good thing going by having been assigned to my class and they knew it. None of them, save for this foolish felon, wanted to mess up their school time by reacting to the baiting remarks of some idiot.

Antonio had something nasty to say to everyone, it didn't matter if you were African American, Latino, Anglo-Saxon, or Native American. Whether you were old, young or disabled, he was an equal opportunity insulter for all. After weeks of his insolence, my patience bad worn thin. But instead of becoming upset, I decided to try counseling him.

I called him to one side during break time and asked him, "Why do you have such a low opinion of everyone? You're constantly going out of your way to insult the other inmates. Haven't you noticed the ugly looks you're getting?"

He just smiled broadly and said, "Mr. Humphries, I have to show you something. Can we go to the law library?"

The library occupied half of the schoolhouse, and the law library was in a special room in the rear. Inmates could come to the library to use law books for researching the penal codes and appellate processes in their everlasting efforts to obtain freedom. These men were called "jailhouse lawyers."

Antonio went straight to the law section, pulled out a book of federal cases, and turned to a particular case where he had been the defendant.

"See, Mr. Humphries, this is why I am the way I am! My case was a federal landmark case," he boasted. "I changed the way the system tries my type of offense! So I'm special and everyone can just kiss my ass if they don't like it!"

He continued bragging about his knowledge of legal matters for several more minutes. When he paused to catch his breath, I reminded him the guard had called for the inmates to leave class. He appeared upset by my interruption, staring me down for a brief moment. Up until that time, I had never had any problems with him.

That day he started on a new drawing, this one an oil portrait of Mickey Mouse. By late afternoon, he finished and placed it on his storage shelf to dry. It was a typical smiling Mickey Mouse, posed with his right hand on his hip and his left hand waving merrily. He was shown in the traditional red shorts, yellow shoes and white gloves. There was nothing unusual about the painting, though I had a class rule: no painting was to be hung on display in the school unless I approved it. I presumed he couldn't do any wrong with a simple painting of little ol' Mickey.

The next school day, he quickly got out his painting and asked for some red, black and white paint. I figured he needed to touch up Mickey's shorts and left him to do what he needed. Minutes later, he was back at my side, asking for permission to hang it up. Since I had seen it the night before, I told him to go ahead. He immediately went to the front of the school and hung it in an obscure place at the front of the schoolhouse, above the air conditioner that was mounted over the front door. Most people wouldn't have noticed it in that spot, unless they were very tall or alert enough to look up.

Now, the air conditioner worked great during the winter months but as the summer approached it mysteriously ceased to function.

That year we were in the middle of yet another hot Texas summer. The front door of the schoolhouse was propped open by huge floor mounted fans blowing at full speed. Anyone coming in knew there would be no air conditioning, so no one bothered to look up after climbing up the three-story-high concrete ramp.

Soon, Antonio returned from hanging his work, his eyes all glazed and glittering again. He made no attempt to start a new project. He neatly sat with a self-satisfied, almost manic, expression. Something wasn't right about that smile. If he had done something I would surely hear about it later, so I decided to keep an eye on him for the rest of the class.

Thirty minutes before the end of class, Marcus, an African American inmate worker, entered the classroom with a very serious expression on his face, his voice quiet but strong.

"Mr. Humphries, you need to go to the front of the schoolhouse. There's a picture that you need to see." Then he turned and glared at the giddy Antonio. Marcus was not beholden to anyone. He was doing time for murder and never talked about himself or his case. But he remembered the Carrasco crisis all too well and how the previous art teacher resigned, so I knew he wanted to keep the art program intact and drama-free.

I went with him to see what the problem was, and sure enough, my student had gotten the best of me. There, hanging high and proud over the building's entrance, was

Antonio's painting of a smiling Mickey Mouse—wearing a Nazi swastika armband.

My jaw dropped and my heart sank. He had used the paints he asked for all right: black for the swastika, white for the circle and red for the armband.

I tore down the painting and made straight for Principal Tracy's office.

"Yes, Jim," Mr. Tracy was puzzled by my abrupt intrusion. "What can I do for you?"

"I want to remove an inmate from my art class."

"Sure, just give his name and TDC number to my bookkeeper. But . . . is everything all right?"

"Soon, sir. Soon it will be!" I was so angry I could barely hide my disgust.

Marcus was waiting outside. He grinned knowingly at me. "Take care of this mess," I barked. "Save the canvas; just wipe that shit off."

"My pleasure, boss." We returned to class with the Mickey painting. Marcus fetched some turpentine and, as he left, shot one last glare at Antonio who was still beaming his knavish grin.

I watched Marcus take care of the offensive painting and then went outside to cool off the best I could in the sweltering sun. As the class was dismissed, I called Antonio over.

"*Why?* Why did you do it?"

"Why not?" He looked puzzled that I even asked. Keeping my temper under control, I informed him his participation in the art class had been terminated, to which he simply shrugged his shoulders with a noncommittal look and turned to leave. As he neared the front door, he turned back in my direction, threw back his head and boomed his maniacal laugh. He cackled all the way to the courtyard below. I wouldn't have been surprised if he didn't survive the length of his sentence.

Somehow he did, though, but not for long.

A year later, as I was getting a haircut from Howard, the prison barber, our conversation turned to the subject of Antonio.

"What a piece of work! You know he'd just mouth off all the time when he was in here, talking about how the world owes him something," Howard said.

"How is he now?" I asked.

"Dead is the word," the barber replied. "After he was paroled, he moved to El Paso and got crossed up with the local drug dealers. Got shot six times in an ambush."

Figures, I thought to myself.

A Different Light

"Phone call for Mr. Hendrickson," called out the guard.

"Sure thing," replied Danny Hendrickson, our teacher of visually impaired inmates replied. He moved rapidly across the floor of our open concept school area to answer a phone call. Scanning with his white cane in a casual, unhurried manner, he rounded my class area and made his way into the teacher's lounge. The way he maneuvered about the world made us wonder if he could actually see. Often visitors would claim that Danny could see at least a little, especially since he looked at right at you when he was speaking.

But Danny Hendrickson was more than blind. He had been born with a rare physical defect where his eyes were unable to stabilize internal pressure. Several operations failed to help him help much. By the age of thirteen, his eyes were about to burst from the pressure, so his family sought the best solution available and that was to remove both eyes and implant artificial ones, surgically attached to his eye muscles.

Sometimes I'd see him walking the four miles to his apartment and I'd ask him if he wanted a lift. "Thanks Jim, but I like to walk," was his usual answer. One day I asked him how he did it, how could he get around without any sight.

"Jim, I'll just have to show you," he replied. "After work, let's a take a walk down FM 247 and you'll see for yourself."

Later that day, we took our walk, chatting as we went along. Finally, Danny stopped and said, "So Jim, you want me to prove what I can do, but I want you to know I don't need anyone's charity. My condition is a matter of circumstance and it's fine by me. But you're a nice fellow and since you asked me so sincerely, I'll oblige. Just remember to keep this to yourself. I'm no sideshow act for anyone's entertainment."

"Don't worry about it, Danny," I assured him.

"Thank you," he said. Then he fell completely silent. He stood there for a moment, not moving, only listening.

"To our right front is a portable toilet for the workmen digging a sewer ditch, standing about fifty feet in front of us." Pointing with his cane, he said, "Over there to the left is the trunk of a large syca-more tree, between us and the curb." To really put him to the test, I decided to ask him to lead the way, to tell me when it was safe to cross the street and where to look for obstructions. He agreed, and as we walked, he went on explaining how his "sonar" worked.

"The environment forms a kind of sonar image in my mind, and based on how I hear sound bounce off objects, I can see where I am going. Losing my eyes improved my sense of smell, too. Smelling enhances everything in the environment. Like that sewer ditch: the softness of earth sounds different from the harshness of asphalt. The freshly turned soil tells me it is a hole but since I can smell it for a while as we walk along, that means the hole is a ditch."

I walked with him several blocks in total amazement, until I said to him, "Danny, I'm going back to my car. I promise to stop worrying when I see you walking home all alone. Hell, you see as well as I do!"

One afternoon, a Windham administrator was visiting my class when he noticed a tall, heavyset African American inmate with extremely thick glasses leaving Danny's visually impaired class with a halting stumble, swinging his cane in front of him.

"How in the world could that crippled, half-blind inmate ever commit a crime and end up in here?" Danny mumbled under his breath to me.

Well, the truth was if you stopped Jerome, the blind inmate, and asked how he was doing, he'd smile and exclaim, "Fine, Jesus, Praise God! I am here, Jesus. I have seen the light and the light is Jesus."

Jerome may have looked harmless but at one time he was one of the toughest, meanest criminals ever to engage in a shootout with the Texas Rangers. Even after he'd been badly wounded, he continued to resist, refusing to drop his weapon. Finally, a Texas Ranger ended the scuffle with a point-blank shot to Jerome's head. Amazingly, not only did he survive the shootout and the headshot, but he found religion too!

"That was the day, praise the Lord, I saw the light," he'd say on many occasions. I suppose that was one way to describe the divine light: coming from a .357 Magnum's blast to the head.

West Texas Nightmare

Carlos, a tall, Chicano inmate, had been my student for several months before he volunteered the story of how he killed his wife. I never attempted to pry into my students' past, but when they wanted to express themselves verbally as well as visually, I did my best to be a good listener.

As Carlos told it, one evening, he had returned home after a few beers with friends at a local cantina. As usual, his wife accused him of chasing other women and being unfaithful. Again and again, he asked her to stop accusing him.

"I only wanted to have a few drinks with my friends," he asserted. "But she kept screaming, kept insulting me! I couldn't take it anymore, you know? I lost it. Don't you ever just lose it and go crazy, Mr. Humphries?"

"Well, I am human," I replied. But—"

"So, you know what I mean then," Carlos interrupted. "I had to shut her up and you know how it is."

"Actually, I don't—" I began, but he wasn't listening.

"I got my pistol and stuck it in her face like this." He held up his right hand, pointing two fingers at me. "I said, 'You better shut up or I'll shoot you!' That just made her even madder, so what could I do?"

"Leave the room?"

"I shot her. Yeah, I shot her until she shut the fuck up. I didn't stop until I ran out of bullets. Oh, man, it all happened so fast but I didn't want to kill her. I just wanted her to stop putting me down. I'm a man, damn it, not a boy! She should have never talked to me like that!"

When the gun was empty, despair and revulsion rushed over Carlos as he realized what he had done. Condemning himself, he phoned the sheriff and waited for him on the front steps of his home. During his trial and his years of incarceration, his dead wife's family continued to visit him. He told me that her family had often warned him about her sharp tongue and hot temper, and that they were not at all surprised he shot her because of how badly she treated him.

With a twenty-year sentence for unpremeditated murder, Carlos wanted to do his time and go on with his life. With credit for good time he would get out earlier, though he couldn't forget the night he killed his wife. Her screams of condemnation and the blasts from his pistol continued to echo in the chambers of his soul.

The beast, created in his anger and loss of control, invaded all his idle and waking moments. To keep it bay, he spent most of his time at his prison job or going to school. Sleep offered little escape from his beast because while others slept, his dreams were devoured and reborn as nightmares.

Though he accepted responsibility for his crime, he came to realize that he too had become a victim of murder. For many transgressors, their guilt remains a heavy yoke they carry for years, even in cases where a victim's family members have moved on with their lives.

Carlos had never tried to draw or paint before coming to my class. Not surprisingly, he wanted to learn to do portraits. Men who miss the people who were a part of their free lives often try to get closer to these memories by drawing or painting portraits. I often discouraged the new students from using personal photos until the student had become more confident in his drawing or painting skills. Practice work based on images from books or magazines, rather than using a photo, was less psychologically threatening for a beginning student.

Soon Carlos developed a good eye for correct proportion, and even a talent for painting people. His first oil painting was painted from a magazine photograph of a young Southwestern Native American bride in contemporary bridal clothing. Finally the day came when I felt he was ready to paint from a personal photo. Just as I had expected, he had only one—of his wife.

She was lovely, with long black hair and lush lips, but she wasn't smiling. She was staring straight at the camera, nary a smile in sight. I asked him if he had taken the picture.

"Yeah," he sighed, "and she was mad at me when I did. She hated me taking pictures of her, so this is the only one I got."

"Well, if you're ready, you may begin painting." But I felt I needed to add something. "But, may I suggest you paint her . . . with a smile?"

This made his eyes light up.

"Start on it, and when you get to the mouth, I'll help make her smile."

We worked on that portrait together for some time. It must have been three or four months before it was complete, every part finished except for her mouth. He would make small changes to it, which usually ended in him being upset. It seemed to be the one part of her he missed most, for it was never good enough. Finally, I had to take over and paint what I thought her smile might've looked like.

"There," adding the last touches. "Now I hope you like . . . " Then I stopped as Carlos, with tears pouring down his cheeks, collapsed into his chair, exhausted by the months of work.

"Thank you, Mr. Humphries. She's . . . she's beautiful," he sobbed. "Just beautiful."

Rodeo Days in the Bull Ring

Mexican Saddle

AS THE TIME OF THE ANNUAL Texas Prison Rodeo approached, I was keeping my students busy painting a multi-paneled mural for the Bull Ring when I noticed Jesus, a young Latino inmate from San Antonio. Jesus had an amazing gift for painting details in a well-balanced composition. The first painting he ever completed was an American Flag, waving in the wind against a blue Texas sky. The painting was from a photograph I took in Austin that windy Sunday morning before Mass, before I returned back to Huntsville to help out Barbara. Every time I looked at it I got the chills as I reminisced of that day: Old Glory's radiant colors, waving high in the heavens, on such a brilliant Easter Morning. I couldn't have done a better job than his. I may have taken the photo but Jesus captured the essence of the moment.

His next painting was based on a black-and-white photograph printed in a Texas history textbook. The photo showed a young Pancho Villa, seated on a horse in a Mexican-style saddle. Villa looked defiantly arrogant with his iconic twin bandoliers across his chest. In the background stood a Spanish mission styled church with large doors.

The only change Jesus made in his painting was the addition of a weeping woman standing beside the doorway of the mission. Jesus requested the addition, which represented his mother crying for his going to prison. He never mentioned why he was in prison, only that "it was not going to happen again."

Jesus was one of my most diligent and talented artists, respected among all prison artists, but none of that mattered when you have a prison official in a wicked humor, looking to boost his own ego.

It was the first Sunday of the Prison Rodeo, and I was at home enjoying a quiet day in my studio. An assistant warden called Jesus down to the Bull Ring and accused him of intentionally painting a pornographic symbol in the Pancho Villa painting. He pointed to the horn of the saddle, claimed that it looked like the head of penis, and demanded my artist admit to the accusation. But Jesus knew better. He had done no wrong and had remembered me telling my students that if they were ever accused of doing something unjust, they should stand by the truth and not panic. Faith in the truth is its own armor.

His courage infuriated the assistant warden, who then ordered the inmate artist to stand in the Bull Ring all afternoon until Warden Cousins from Ellis, could get there and identify the saddle as an authentic Mexican design. The assistant warden knew I was responsible for the design and installation of the mural, but he didn't bother to call me at home, which was only five miles away.

People see what they want to in a work of art. This assistant warden apparently had never seen a Mexican-style saddle, so he was convinced that the saddle's horn was meant as a phallic insult. His beast was feeding off his own megalomania, which had mistakenly convinced him that it was right to make someone suffer until he could prove his point.

When Warden Cousins arrived, the assistant warden took him to the painting and asked if that was an actual Mexican saddle horn. "Why, yes it is," Warden Cousins replied. The Warden had a friend who owned a couple of mustangs and who loved these types of saddles. And, having ridden on one himself, Warden Cousins could say for sure the inmate had it painted right. The assistant warden swallowed his pride and, without any apology, dismissed Jesus after having forced him to stand for hours in the Bull Ring.

The next day Jesus told me the whole story when we ran into each other on the schoolhouse ramp. He expressed sincere gratitude for my advice.

"If you hadn't told me to keep cool and stand my ground, I might've been in solitary right now instead of at school," he informed me. "I was stuck in there for so long, my legs were aching from standing but I stayed strong, just like you said."

"I'm glad you held your own."

"Too bad you weren't there to seen how embarrassed he got when Warden Cousins told him that I was right!"

Vietnam Veteran

Cal was an African American inmate artist from South Dallas, Texas. Before Walls, he had completed two tours of duty in Vietnam as a door gunner on an Army helicopter. A quiet, easy-going young man, he had the classic demeanor of an adept artist.

Not long after he returned from Vietnam, his life spun out of control. From the jungle of his emotions, the beast crawled out to destroy his character in the eyes of his community. His wife abruptly left him, moving far away. As anger and anxiety blinded Cal, he was seized with the idea that he had to find money quickly to buy a plane ticket so he could follow her. He took his service pistol and attempted to rob the nearest convenience store. What's odd is he kept apologizing to the store clerk for having to rob them.

"It went like this," Cal told me. "'Sir, I'm sorry but I just have to do this. You know how it is when your wife wants to leave you and fly away.' But that was my mistake. The police were waiting for me at the airport."

This was his first felony offense. His only prior was for arguing with a police officer about a traffic violation. I didn't care much about his crime, though he did intrigue me because he seemed different from the other inmates, not to mention being sublimely artistic.

His work, both drawing and painting, was of professional quality. I used his talent for painting the human figures and portraitures in three paintings for the Bull Ring mural: "Football in Texas," "Toddler with Pup," and "We, the People." "Football in Texas" depicted the rivalry between the University of Texas and Texas A & M University. "Toddler with a Pup" captured the inmates' feelings and memories of their homes and families. "We, the People" was a black and white photo of a man and woman in the streets of the free world, among an interlocking composition of images that revealed their desires for

a better future. Both of them seemed poised with anticipation that something good was going to happen, and they were ready for it.

He let his brush speak volumes for him, churning out exquisite paintings every week. One day he came to me with a letter from his mother. In the letter she asked him to ask me to write the parole board on his behalf. Normally, I would be skeptical: This might be another con game. But because Cal was a Vietnam vet and a talented artist, I decided to help him. It would be the first and last time that I would write the parole board on behalf of any of my students.

In a few months he was paroled. I was happy to have been part of his freedom, but this delight was short-lived. It hadn't been long when I saw him in the unit craft shop, shuffling about by him self. I couldn't believe my eyes! I ran over and asked him if he was back on a parole violation.

"No, it's a new case," he replied, looking defeated. "And it's sixty-five years this time, but I'm innocent!"

I prayed that he was, not for his sake but mine. The thought passed through my mind that I had assisted in gaining this man's freedom. And what did he do just months later? Commit another crime.

Cowboy Biker

Lloyd, a giant of an inmate, burst into my art class, mad as hell. With great strides, he made a beeline toward the bookshelves. Some students took notice but most didn't bother looking up. Lloyd clambered up the shelves, his massive weight causing them to break. On the wall above the bookshelves hung my students' finished artwork, including some of his.

He grabbed only for his works of art, ripping them off the wall and throwing them to the ground. Lloyd then leapt from the shelves and landed with a loud thud. Growling through grinding teeth, he tore his paintings to pieces. By now, we all were looking at him. He glared right back at us, literally foaming at the mouth. I snuck out when he wasn't looking and hurried to the nearest security officer. I think my expression said enough, because he took off with me without us saying a word.

As we reached the classroom, we slowed to a walk to at least give the impression we had things under control. Once inside, the guard walked over to where Lloyd was still throwing his fit and said gruffly, "Okay now, I think you've had enough. Now, let's go!"

The anger disappeared instantly from Lloyd's face. "Yes, boss," he replied, looking defeated. Gone was his flaming glare and foaming lips as the guard led him off to solitary.

Class continued with no discussion of the incident. *Just another day at Walls,* I thought. Before I even asked, inmate workers replaced the broken shelves, straightened the scattered books and returned to their regular duties. I collected Lloyd's artwork he had left on a table and stored it in a safe place, knowing he'd want to continue his projects.

Lloyd spent three days in solitary confinement as a result of that incident. The next time I saw him in class, he had been cut down to size.

"Mr. Humphries," he said in his most chastened tone, "I have to apologize for my outburst. I bear no hard feelings toward you for sending me to solitary. If it's okay by you, may I come back to class?"

"Of course you can," I answered. "Besides, I knew you weren't really angry with me."

A teacher must be consistent and fair with classroom management, especially where discipline is concerned. In a correctional education classroom this is especially important because the teacher must always be in charge. Unlike schools in the free world, a simple classroom behavioral problem in prison can lead to the death of an inmate. Luckily, acts of violence against teachers very seldom occur in Texas prisons. Only under the most severe circumstances, like the Carrasco siege, would any teacher feel they were in personal danger.

In Texas, any employee who's taken in a hostage situation has zero negotiation value. All negotiations are made with the safety of the people of the State of Texas in consideration. Just because a hostage is a TDC or Windham employee, male or female, warden or schoolteacher, makes no difference to the negotiators. Therefore, teachers must take their classroom management with utmost seriousness, not only for their safety, but in order to develop mutual respect between themselves and their students.

For all of his size and occasional grumbles, Lloyd was an excellent artist. The truth is, though, I had no idea what he might do next. Nevertheless, I needed him to finish his painting of A.J. Foyt's Indy 500 racecar for the Bull Ring mural. He had shown me photos of his life in the free world, of him with his huge beard sitting astride his Harley-Davidson. He considered himself a sort of cowboy: a loner because he didn't wear patches to show he was a member of any motorcycle gang or club.

"Those guys tell you who to associate with, what to wear or what not to, and where you can ride," he said. "Hell, I ride for me! I'm a modern cowboy with horse made of chrome. And, I like it that way!"

Then came the day when he told me the path he'd taken to prison. Raised in Boston, Massachusetts, by a blue collar Irish family, Lloyd turned to his fists whenever any of the neighborhood kids got on his nerves. His bad temper landed him in prison for aggravated assault before his twentieth birthday.

Lloyd's family moved to East Texas while he was locked up, not bothering to tell him where they'd settled. After he was paroled, a friend was nice enough to give him their address. When he arrived in Texas, things did not get any better. While employed in his father's auto dealership, he got into trouble again.

"I was minding my own business," he recalled, "just eating my Sonic burger and fries on my Harley, when this yuppie prick drove up beside me in a flashy Alfa-Romeo convertible, trying to look cool for his lady friend. It would've been cool with me but he kept staring at me, looking all high and mighty. Mr. Humphries, I don't take kindly to people staring me down, especially when I'm enjoying my lunch, so I says to him, 'What the hell you looking at?' He just sat there all smug and sneered, 'At nothing. Just mind your own business and keep eating your burger on that little scooter, you clown!' Oh boy, I got so mad I almost choked on a French fry!"

"So he called you a clown," I said, trying not to laugh.

Looking at me with cold eyes, he replied, "No one disrespects me or my Harley! He had it coming and his lady friend knew it."

More words were passed and soon the cowboy biker lost control. Leaping on the hood of the Alfa, he began to stomp dents with his feet and smash the windshield with his gloved fists. The yuppie and his lady were frozen by fear, which only fueled Lloyd's beast. He jumped off the car, smashing on the fenders, doors, and anything else he could reach. Snapping out of his panic, the driver slammed the Alfa into reverse and sped away as quickly as it could go.

Later that afternoon while working in his father's body shop, our cowboy saw the driver of the smashed Alfa talking to the body shop supervisor. He tried to remain unnoticed amid the car parts, but soon afterward a deputy sheriff walked up to him. He knew his time had come again. The beast had claimed years of his life once again, for the next shop he'd work in would be Huntsville's prison auto repair shop.

One afternoon after class was over, I asked Lloyd, "What has hurt you the most during your life?" He turned partially away and gave a painful, forced grin that showed his missing front tooth.

"When I was in school, my parents always went to see my sister perform in plays and concerts, but never came to see me play football. Everything in our family seemed to be for her benefit. But nothing was ever done for me."

He slumped over and continued: "One day at practice, I got hit real hard by a fullback. Knocked the wind out of me, and cost me my front tooth. When my mom and dad saw me without my tooth, they just stared at me with disgust, calling me names and saying things like I deserved it for playing football."

"Did they at least take you to get checked out?"

"Naw. I suppose they didn't see any need to," he grumbled. "I was always fighting and getting hurt. Figured they knew I was gonna lose a tooth someday. It didn't matter, because that was when I knew I had to fend for myself."

Weeks later, I saw him wave at me from under his welding mask, beckoning me to join him. The closer I got, the more I noticed he was smiling. He grinned and pointed to the space where missing tooth would be. There nestled between the central incisors and canine, was a gleaming gold tooth, encrusted with a single diamond set in the center.

"Nice touch, but where'd you get that?" I asked.

"I never wore this until today because I was afraid I'd lose it or it would get stolen."

"So, is there something special about today?"

"You bet your ass today's special," Lloyd boasted. "I just got paroled! Tomorrow, I'll be a free man!"

"I wish you all the luck. And please, don't let me see you in here again."

"Thanks, Mr. Humphries. And you can count in it. I'm never coming back to this place."

"I'll see you when I see you," I said. And I never did see him at Walls again.

Several months later, I stopped by a Kroger's supermarket in Conroe to purchase some choice cuts. As I was examining the sirloins, a voice behind me said, "Are you having a hard time there?" I turned and there was Lloyd himself, in full western gear, down to the snakeskin boots and ten gallon hat.

He smiled a gold tooth grin, and told me his life has never been better. He told me being in prison had no effect on him but that our friendship did. He also revealed that his artwork had helped him sort out some issues.

"That's why I tore up my paintings that day. I wanted to get rid of the man I once was. And it worked! During those three days in solitary, I decided my life needed a change, so I started by making amends with you. And let me tell you, it meant a lot that you didn't judge me for acting all crazy."

"Hey, water under the bridge. It's good to see you've given up on the whole lonesome biker life."

"What? No way, man! I'm not *that* crazy!"

A Native American Point of View

I would usually allow new students to draw without making any attempts to help them, other than to provide art supplies. But there was one student who became an exception to that rule.

I noticed Rudy was drawing with his nose only millimeters from the paper, his head almost flat on his desk. I moved closer to see what he was drawing. He raised his head and looked at me, expressionless and silent. I'm sorry to recall that I winced at the sight of him. The left side of his head was mangled and deformed, mashed in around the temple and across the outside edge of his left eye. At first I thought he might be Latino but that was incorrect. He was a Navajo. You could see the years of a hard life lived had weathered his face almost to where it likened the deep red rocks of Arizona's Oak Creek Canyon. Half his face was ruined beyond repair, while the other side was rugged beyond his years.

"May I see what you're drawing?" I asked as politely as I could. Without a word, he picked it up and handed it over. Using only pencil and a piece of spiral notebook paper, he had drawn a montage of Native American imagery. I had seen similar work done before, but usually it was copied from the pages of *Southwest Art* magazine.

So I asked him, "What's your source for your drawing?"

A faint smile flashed across his face as he replied, "My imagination."

And Rudy wasn't lying. Because of the quality of draftsmanship, composition, and probable authentic detail, I was amazed this inmate was in my class. He'd created all of this beautiful work on plain notebook paper, with his face half an inch off the surface.

"Do you have any eyeglasses?" I asked.

"No."

"Would you like a pair? It would surely help you to see better."

He sat in silence for a moment, staring at nothing. I stood there feeling awkward, not knowing if I should apologize or just leave him be. Finally, he answered at a slow, deliberate pace.

"My left eye . . . does not see . . . I was young . . . a drunk white man . . . in a pickup . . . ran over my head . . . only my right eye can see . . . and not very well."

He sighed and sat there for a moment, lost in his memories. "I . . . I would like to see better," he slowly replied, as if it was difficult to admit he needed my help. He wasn't friendly to anyone and rarely spoke in complete sentences. I knew I had to do something.

"You do good work, Rudy. I'll see what I can do for you," I told him. "May I borrow this drawing for a few minutes?"

He nodded. I then dashed over to our new Principal Thompson's office where I found him behind stacks of paperwork.

"Excuse me, sir—"

"*Yes*," the principal snapped from behind a pile of files. "Oh! Jim, it's you. I'm sorry, didn't see you over these, uh . . . what can I do for you?"

"Mr. Thompson, I have something I want you to see." I handed him the drawing. "The inmate who drew that has only one working eye. The other . . . let's just say it doesn't work anymore. Anyway, he has a natural talent for drawing but he can barely see. Think of how much better he'd be if he had a good pair of glasses! So, can we help him?"

He sat there, staring at the picture while picking at loose chads left on the page. Principal Thompson was shrewd and decisive, so the patience he was showing now seemed a little unusual. I took the hint, and stood silently at parade rest. Without a word, Mr. Thompson phoned the hospital, exchanged some short words, and hung up. Then he pulled out a spiral notebook of his own, wrote something quick, and looked up at me.

"We're talking about the inmate with half a face, right?" he asked. "You know, he never gives anyone the time of day. But you seem to think he's important enough for special treatment, and I can't refuse an honest man like yourself some charity work."

He ripped the page from the spiral notebook, folded it twice and continued picking at the chads on the drawing.

"Jim, I'm going to let you handle this one for us," he stated, handing me the note. "Give him this and send him to the hospital's eye clinic. They'll be waiting for him."

"Mr. Thompson, um, the drawing?"

"Oh, right," he said, taking one more long look at it. "Sorry."

I walked back to my class and quietly told Rudy the news as I gave him his drawing back. His eyes opened wide, with a look of disbelief. I smiled and gave him a reassuring nod. Slowly he rose to his feet, folded his drawing into his pocket, and left.

Two weeks passed. Class sessions passed without incident. Then one day Rudy walked into the classroom wearing a pair of thick, black plastic-framed glasses, and a big grin. After collecting his supplies, he walked straight up to me and said words I never would forget:

"Thank you. You are the only white man who has ever helped me."

"You're welcome."

Now he could work at a normal distance when drawing or painting. And paint he did! I cannot take any credit for teaching him anything, because the treatment department made it possible for him to have the proper vision correction. He was very proud that he was now able to see with his good eye. Nothing could help the eye that had been crushed, so he made the good eye do double duty. When I asked him if he would be interested in helping on the Bull Ring mural project, he answered with a quiet but firm, "Yes!"

The first assignment that he chose was a two-feet-by-six-feet portrait of the undefeated Comanche chief, Quanah Parker. The black-and-white historical photo we used as our basic reference had a teepee in the background. My Navajo inmate artist requested to make a few changes and I approved. First, since he was interpreting the photo in color, he wanted to show a southwest desert background with a lot of blue sky. Then he wanted to change Chief Parker's moccasins to the Sioux Indian style, worn during the massacre at Wounded Knee. Third, he wanted to intensify the expression of Chief Quanah's hands and face.

He executed his vision masterfully. The completed painting was eerie to look at: You could feel Chief Quanah's eyes following you. The next work Rudy did was of a cowboy riding a bucking bronco. The composition created a sense of tension between horse and rider. The consistent detail he brought out amplified the strength of the composition and enhanced its expression. It was brilliant.

The day I hung his buckaroo painting, I happened upon Principal Thompson staring at the Quanah Parker painting. I didn't want to bother him, so I just hung up the buckaroo piece next to the Chief. Mr. Thompson stood silently, looking at the cowboy and horse, both of them in a struggle for dominance.

As I was leaving, he called out, "These are . . . his, right?"

"Yes, sir. Yes they are."

"You were right, Jim," he nodded. He was now looking at the buckaroo. "He's quite the artist."

Although by nature a quiet person, Rudy spoke through his work in thundering volumes of emotion. He never discussed himself,

his family, the weather or even the time of day. When I approached him as he was painting, he'd simply stop and slowly step back in silence, understanding I wanted to see his progress. I'd make a few suggestions and always complimented him on the excellent quality of his work. He would look at me through his black-rimmed glasses, and sometimes give me a slight but thoroughly satisfied grin. He never said a word unless he had a question. He exhibited the most self-control of any inmate, of any person, that I have ever met. With a little kindness from Principal Thompson and me, and a little faith from us all, he had overcome the beast that had made it impossible for him to trust the white man.

After the mural project was completed, I received permission to host a soft drink and cake get-together with my inmate artists. My wife, Celeste, baked a special cake in the shape of a large chocolate palette. It contained the name of every inmate who had worked on the mural project, each name drawn in a different color. I wanted to show my appreciation for their eight months of hard work.

But Rudy didn't show up.

And I never saw him again.

I later learned that the Parole Board granted him early release, so he spent his last days at Walls drawing pictures alone. I was thankful to witness those few, precious weeks of uncanny creativity. Drawing on the memory of his people, Rudy had left us all a gift to enjoy for years to come.

And if that was his way of saying thank you for a simple yet precious pair of TDC eyeglasses, so be it. Wherever he is and whatever he's doing, I hope he's enjoying the deep blue of an Arizona sky and the song of the desert wind.

A<small>RT</small> T<small>HERAPY</small>

Cruel Joke

IN MARCH OF 1979, Dr. Jeff White, our new clinical psychologist arrived at Walls. His assistant, Mr. Habib, was a psychologist from Algiers. Mr. Habib was short and slightly built, with thick curly hair and a heavy Arabic accent. Extremely thin, almost delicate in appearance, he brought an interesting intensity and dedication to his work. Unfortunately, he didn't have much of a sense of humor. By contrast, Dr. White was tall, athletic and had an excellent sense of humor. We sometimes referred to them as the Mutt and Jeff of the treatment center, but were careful not to say that around Mr. Habib.

Mr. Habib set up a temporary bio-feedback clinic in two vacant cells on the top run of A-block: one for his lab and one for his office. One afternoon Dr. White decided to play a little joke on Mr. Habib by having him "accidentally" locked inside his makeshift office.

"Hello? Somebody! Let me out! You have made a big mistake!" Mr. Habib called out with a rising note of panic. I was on the lower run when I saw him desperately looking off to his left, to the area where the doors for the upper run of A-block were controlled. I thought about helping him, but then I saw Dr. White casually strolling up the run with a mischievous snicker.

"Pardon me! I'm in here! Let me out! Let me out!" His shrill pleas were now painfully loud. Then Dr. White appeared.

"Mr. Habib, now why are you locked in there? I thought you'd gone home." Looking around curiously, Dr. White continued, "Are you trying out a new experiment?"

"Jeff! You not play on me! You let me out!" When Mr. Habib got upset, his command of English suffered.

Dr. White signaled the guard, who freed Mr. Habib. As Mr. Habib came out of his office, he gave Dr. White a hard, penetrating stare, turned on his heel and stomped off. It was a cruel joke, but everyone who was new suffered a little teasing at TDC. It took a couple of days before Mr. Habib cooled down and became a good sport about it.

Not long after, I was back teaching in the treatment center, now under the auspices of Dr. White and his staff. They gave me specific instructions on how I would log my work with the psychiatric patients. I was glad to have a second opportunity to continue this pioneer project in prison art therapy.

Art therapy was still a fledgling branch of psychotherapy during the 1970s, but thanks to the prior studies into psychotic art by researchers Erich Guttmann, Walter Maclay, and Francis Reitman, we had some notion of what to look for. (By 1982, researchers Barry M. Cohen and Barbara Lesowitz would develop the Diagnostic Drawing Series, a widely used art therapy assessment that is used today by numerous art therapists.)

Short Trip to Insanity

I had first met Taylor, a young, African American inmate, in my regular art class. He slowly moved around, as if in a permanent daydreamer's haze. He was a thin, angular man with an aloof attitude and absurd manner of dress who made no attempt to mingle with the other inmates. One other thing about him was peculiar: He always wore a pair of sunglasses that he never took off.

No art student, free world or inmate, would attempt to learn to mix color while wearing sunglasses, unless the person had a severe medical problem or was just blind. One day I asked Taylor, "Have you tried to see what colors look like without your sunglasses?" He stopped what he was doing and tilted his head back, staring at the ceiling through dark plastic discs.

"What difference would it make?" he asked, staring at nothing.

"Difference?" I pardoned his seemingly insolent reply. "Sunglasses alter how you see the world. Without them, you would see how to shade or lighten the mixtures of complimentary colors to create a variety of neutrals. For that one thing, neutrals are necessary if you want to learn to paint portraits."

"Boss, I have *fifty years* to learn," he snapped back. "Do you think that'll be plenty of time?"

Before I could muster a reply, he went off on a tangent, telling his story as if I had pushed the play button on an old and painful recording.

"Do you think it's fair to get *fifty years* for something you didn't do?"

"You mean to tell me you're here by mistake?"

"Yeah, man," he shot back. "I didn't kill that man. My cousin did. I just minded my own business while he did all the killing."

"Doesn't that make you an accessory to murder?" I asked, preparing for the extended, "justified rationalization speech" most inmates have ready in these situations. His voice lowered to a monotonous drone as he began to detail his case.

"My cousin and I was drivin' home from a party. He just done some time and was on parole, so we were out celebratin'. We was drinkin' beer and smokin' weed, when we saw this car by road with its hood up, and two pretty girls standing around, watching another man trying to fix the car. I know a thing or two about cars, so we stopped to help. We was thinkin' we could help them girls, and maybe they'd take a likin' to us. So my cousin told me to get my tools out the back and see what I could do with the engine, while he gone off to talk to them girls."

"Now, I don't know what he said or did, 'cuz before I could tell what was goin' on, him and that other man were fightin'. Then my cousin grabs a screwdriver out of my toolbox and stabs the man a whole bunch of times. But I didn't see any of this! All I heard was those girls screamin'! Screamin' so much I couldn't think straight. The next thing I know, my cousin throws my screwdriver back in my toolbox and said, 'Let's get out of here.' I told him I couldn't get their engine goin' but he said 'forget it and come on.' But those girls just kept a-screamin'. That's when I saw the man, lyin' on the roadside, all bloody."

"We got into our car and drove home. My cousin told me to keep quiet about what happened. Mama knew something was wrong, so she kept askin' until I told her. Man, she started cryin', sayin' things like 'You didn't kill anyone but they gonna come lookin' for you. Those girls done take down his license number, so I know they're calling the sheriff too. So I'm gonna call him first and see that you turn yourself in.' I told Mama I wasn't sure and I didn't want to go to prison but she said, 'You didn't do anything to that man! You minded your own business.'"

"So the deputy came and I surrendered peacefully. I thought he was just gonna to take my statement and send me home, but no. They charged me with accessory to murder! I didn't do anything! I was high on weed, man, and I was just tryin' to help those girls, but I couldn't get their engine goin'. My cousin killed that man, not me. So why did they *charge me* with something I didn't do? They say I should've tried to stop my cousin but why? It was none of my business. My cousin been to prison, he knew right from wrong. It was none of my business, man, *none of my business*! They say he got less time than me. *How?* Man, I didn't kill nobody!"

He continued to go over the same issue, over and over, until his voice trailed off into silence. Then he just sat there, staring through his dark sunglasses at nothing. When the class was over, he left, walking out mechanically, as though he really didn't know where he was going or why. A week later he dropped out of art class.

The next time I saw Taylor, he was in the treatment center. During an art therapy session with some patients, I caught a glimpse of a man wearing sunglasses, sitting in his cell. And it was Taylor. I tried to say hello but it was useless. He just sat there, staring into space. I asked the guard what his problem was.

"Oh, him," answered the guard. "Yeah, he's a vegetable. Totally withdrawn. Won't speak to anyone, not even the doctors. Just sits all day and night with his sunglasses on, looking at the wall. And now administration says he might be a suicide risk."

I could almost hear the beast gnawing on that young inmate's bones.

Dogs and Flowers

On my next visit to the treatment center, I found myself instructing Mike, an older inmate who was under heavy sedation. Mike appeared to be in his sixties. He sat down at the table and gently rocked back and forth, dribbling drool all over his shirt. In front of him and the three other patients were laid out drawing boards, papers and my usual cigar box full of crayons.

During the first session, he filled his drawing paper with what he called "Dog and Flowers." His dog was quite unique, to say the least. Picture a simple, childish silhouette of a dog, showing four legs, a tail, and pointed ears with no eyes. Now imagine an open mouth, with scores of sharp teeth that covered not only the upper and lower jaw, but also extended around the entire outline of the animal, like an aura of incisors. The perimeter of teeth gave his dog an eerie viciousness. It literally glowed with a halo of fangs.

The flowers were always done with as many colors as he could find in the cigar box. The first drawing showed a couple flowers doodled in a far corner of the page. As the days turned into weeks, the flowers began to grow from that little corner and cover more of the page, as the dog gradually lost teeth and became smaller. Then the day came when the entire page was covered with flowers.

"What happened to the dog?" I asked.

"No more dogs. Only flowers," he said gruffly.

The doctors decreased his sedative dosage, and as the weeks progressed, he became more lucid, even friendly. When the dogs were gone, so were his drooling vacant stares and the rocking back and forth. I could see his beast in that black-toothed animal, but his spirit had proved indomitable. Now, in his work, colorful flowerbeds flourished everywhere.

Patients tend to repeat symbols unique only to them in predictable patterns, I learned. I identified fifteen distinct categories of symbols and logged my observations of each patient's work according to the symbol type and date created. These patient logs provided chronological insight into how they thought, felt and perceived the world and their role in it. I presented my findings to the clinical psychologist, who warmly received and encouraged my work.

"Jim, you're a true man of science," praised Dr. White. I was no glutton for flattery, but it made me feel proud of doing something that made measurable differences in the lives of these men.

Most of the inmates from my regular art classes refused to help me categorize the patients' work. They claimed that working with the patient drawings was too depressing. Prison was hard enough, so none of them wanted a reminder on how much worse life can be. I sympathized completely. Every day, I left the treatment center also feeling downcast, as if I was covered in a kind of spiritual debris. It weighed heavy on my soul to see these men reduced to slobbering wretches.

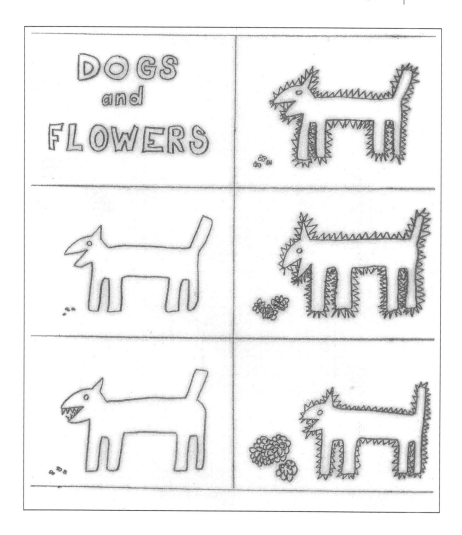

Fortunately, I had a solution to combat my depression: attending Daily Mass. Those afternoons I dragged my heavy and heartbroken body into church, and kneeled to pray for what seemed like hours. Some days were worse than others: I would be so deep in prayer that Mass would end without me even noticing. Only the gentle touch of the deacon's hand on my shoulder pulled me out of my prayer. I'd look up at him, cheeks wet from tears, despondent. I remember how he'd kneel, take me in his arms, and tell me that what I was doing

was right. Lifting me to my feet, he'd repeat this verse to me, from Matthew 25:40:

"Inasmuch as ye have done it unto one of the least of these my brethren, ye have done it unto me."

Thanks to this spiritual renewal, my psychic armor was able to stand up to another day of peering into the dark depths of man's agony. I knew the Spirit of Christ was walking with me. I could lay my daily problems and horrors at his feet and He would lift me up.

Young Frankenstein

Albert was deathly silent: rarely a word and nary a smile—picture what Mary Shelley's monster might look like if he actually existed. Minus the electrodes protruding from his neck, gangrened skin and face stitches, Albert could've walked right out of Victor Frankenstein's laboratory. He was colossal, with broad shoulders, greasy black hair, and glassy eyes behind black-rimmed glasses. He lumbered about in a heavy-footed manner, stooped and slumping, knocking over things wherever he went.

A treatment center guard saw the look on my face the moment I saw this towering man and remarked, "Pretty amazing, huh?"

"Yes," I answered. "I've never . . . that man is . . . wow."

"Yup, he's a big fella. Dangerous too! He committed what the law calls an over-kill. The victim's body was slashed up into little pieces. It was so awful the police couldn't bear the sight of it. Made four deputies and a sergeant lose their lunch. And the blood was just everywhere. But for some reason, he piled all her bits and pieces into a stack in the middle of the kitchen, then covered it with flour and sugar."

"That's horrible!" I was losing my appetite and tried to cut his story short. "Well, I think I've heard—"

But the guard wasn't finished. Once again, I was a captive audience.

"The police found him sitting on the poor lady's front porch, covered in blood. Didn't seem to notice nor mind either. And they had a task just trying to take him in! He couldn't fit into any of the cars, and there weren't big enough cuffs to get around his wrists, so the deputies had to wait for the paddy wagon. Hell, he barely fits in our biggest cells!"

"So how'd he end up here?"

"Oh yeah, you weren't here when it all happened. Well, some of the inmates tried making fun of him, calling him 'Frankenstein,' but he didn't take kindly to that sort of treatment. So one day at chow they caught him strangling not one but two inmates at the same time! Lemmi tell ya, that fella got the death grip! He can wrap his paws around your neck and crush it like a Dixie cup! Took eight guards and a sedative shot to stop him from killing those idiots. Lucky for us, he woke up just after we got him into a treatment cell. Yeah, he's a handful."

To be honest, I don't know how much of this story was embellished fact or outrageous fantasy, but I did know this man was deeply disturbed.

He was also on my roster for the next art therapy session.

Naturally, when he and my other seven art therapy students sat down for their first day in their treatment session, I was more than a bit anxious. The session began in the usual fashion, by laying out bond papers, drawing boards, and my trusty cigar box of Crayolas. I told them to pick a color of crayon and draw any shape they wanted. They could choose as many colors as they wanted. I demonstrated how to manipulate the crayon, using the edge of the tip for narrow lines or the crayon's side for broad lines. Albert rummaged through the box, fisted a purple crayon, and proceeded to press the crayon hard against the paper, effectively crushing it completely. I asked him if I could help, but he just grunted back. Unnerved, I took his arm gently and showed him how to hold the crayon. This was my first breakthrough.

As I described earlier, I had first tried to get the patients to draw specific things from magazine photos, such as birds or trees. But that was a dismal failure. To them, the photo represented a standard to be judged by, which led to insurmountable protest. So I let them draw whatever came from their imagination. Albert began to produce colorful abstract designs using jagged broad lines. After each round of drawing, I collected them and tried to talk about each one with the rest of the group, though verbal interaction was nearly impossible.

Then the day came when I heard the giant speak. I was having a Q&A about the day's drawings with the class when I heard a guttural, low voice moan, "Blue sea." It was Albert, talking about his picture of randomly colored shapes on a blue background. It caught me off guard, so I asked him to repeat what he'd said.

"Blue sea," he grunted.

"In your drawing?" I asked. "Oh yes, I do see it! It is very blue."

"Blue sea."

"Yes, I see it now. What else can you tell us about your picture?" I asked, but he didn't answer. After two months of work, I obtained not only some artwork but also two words from a complete mute!

I believed the classes were a success in this way, not only because the patients seemed to enjoy their artwork, but also because it helped the psychiatrists look for ways to help the patients regain sanity and function normally.

The sessions were going fine until the day ginger-haired patient named Lyle showed up. From the moment he came out of his cell, I knew he'd be trouble. As he sat down, he looked up at Albert, who sat much taller.

"You sure are big!" exclaimed Lyle. "Why are you here? Don't you belong in a zoo or something? Don't you know it's rude to stare at people?" Frankenstein crushed a crayon in his hand without any change in his facial express. I had to act fast.

"Guard! Please escort this patient back to his cell." Not wanting to call attention to Albert, I added, "And after that, please take care of the rest of the class. Class is over for today."

Lyle had no idea how close he'd come to getting killed. As for me, no way could I risk a confrontation that would have ended with Lyle's brains and red hair strewn all over the floor.

Windows into the Soul

Self-mutilation: an unfortunate act of desperation with oneself as the victim. Many of my students had been such victims. Most of these were attempted suicides, efforts to either stop the beast from devouring their soul or to get help in coping with their nightmare daily existence.

As I read the medical history of my treatment center students, a common thread went through most of the cases. All of them were suicide-prone, and most shared the common diagnosis: schizophrenia. Their drawings began to fall into fifteen categories: religious symbols, abstract designs, houses, hands, modes of transportation, universal symbols (heart, star, crescent), geometric forms (circle, triangle, square), weapons, graves, flowers, people (usually stick people), animals, landscapes, cityscapes, and the rare pictorial from prison life. In time, I collected approximately six thousand of these drawings, all categorized by date and symbol.

Each work became a window into a soul, a labyrinth that twisted through the unknown forces of a condemned man's psyche. Often their significance was deciphered too late because the meaning only became apparent when all of a patient's drawings were viewed postmortem. Usually it was their final work before they died that provided the key that solved the riddle of their insanity.

Take the case of my student Reginald: At twenty years old, this African American inmate went into a major panic attack when he was sentenced to fifteen years at Ferguson. The doctors sent him to the treatment center for observation after he stopped talking and eating. When he began attending my art therapy sessions, his attitude changed for the better. He smiled all the time.

Though a cheerful fellow, he was very serious about his drawing. He drew his favorite symbol every class: a Rolls Royce. Drawn in a simple childlike manner, and always facing to the left, the car provided a clue to who he was. As the weeks moved into months, he added details and characteristics to his Rolls.

But one day he reversed the direction of the car, added a steering wheel, then a driver, who he identified as himself. Then he added a stop sign in front of the car, but the doors were gone, as were the door latches. His last drawing was a double tracing of his hands, overlapping as if to ward something off or to shield him from an assault. I asked him why he drew that.

He smiled and said, "Oh, I just got discharged back to the Ferguson Unit. Docs say I'm all better now."

In the treatment center the patients were allowed wear a one-piece white jump suit at most. Sometimes they were only allowed to wear boxer shorts or, if necessary, required to wear nothing if they were considered a suicide risk. I mention this because shortly after Reginald returned to Ferguson, he hanged himself with his TDC-issued belt.

This news gave me deep pangs of frustration. I went back to his drawings and studied them. I'm no psychiatrist but I surmised that his work indicated he made a decision to end his life he prior to being discharged to Ferguson. The double tracing of his hands and the abrupt change in the way he drew the Rolls Royce showed a possible decision to change something in his life. I noticed this sudden change in the symbols drawn by other patients, before they too were found dead from suicide after being released into the general prison population.

My findings were not conclusive enough to be a reliable indicator of a probable suicide. But I did think they warranted attention, so I brought them to the psychologists for their consideration.

"Hmmm, that's interesting, Mr. Humphries. Quite interesting," they said, and left it at that.

A Rudolph Christmas

There was never any Christmas cheer in the treatment center. During the last class before Christmas break, I could see that everything had become too much of a routine. Green shirts were doling out medications in white paper cups and checking to see if the meds were swallowed, as the patients and I went through the motions of just another week.

Art therapy is helpful to inmates

By CAROLYN HART
SHSU News Staff

There is only one thing that Jim Humphries has in common with Mr. and Mrs. John Hunt. They both work with emotionally disturbed people.

In Humphries case, the patients are prisoners who cannot function with other Texas Department of Corrections inmates. The Hunts work with children.

Humphries, art therapist with TDC spoke on "Art Therapy in a Correctional Environment: Felony Offenders in a Psychiatric Treatment Center."

He is the only art therapist in the country who works in cell blocks with the prisoners. Other art therapists work in psychiatric centers.

His "patients" usually show self-punishment (often self-mutilation and suicide), and seldom violence towards other inmates.

"Most of them are young with short sentences, who cannot accept being in prison," said Humphries.

According to Humphries, a drawing will show if a man is faking mental illness or not.

When asked to draw houses, Humphries has found that severe schizophrenics draw houses that are sometimes see-through, with three sides showing at once, something that is impossible with a four-walled house.

Most of the prisoners put chimneys on their house drawings. Even the absence or presence of smoke from the chimneys is indicative, according to Humphries.

"The presence of birds is also significant," said Humphries. "If you ask them what kind of birds they are, they usually say buzzards, which can be regarded as a symbol of death."

The Hunts (Hunt serves as administrator and chaplain at the Angie Nall Hospital for Learning Disabilities in Beaumont, and Mrs. Hunt serves as assistant director) spoke on "Learning Disabilities Which Lead to Delinquency."

They deal with problem children between the ages of 5 and 21, and feel that emotional, social, and physical problems cannot be separated, and usually believe the cause is organic.

"We never have a conference with just one parent," said Mrs. Hunt. "It takes the cooperation of both if a child is to make it. If there is only one parent, we insist that someone come with him or her. In most cases, it's good for the child to be there."

She has found that apathetic students are the hardest to work with. "It's a defense they throw up," she said.

A-Block seemed unusually quiet for a Thursday. No one was screaming or hanging from the bars. Even the inmate who was always pacing the floor and flushing the commode at every turn was now calmly lying on his bunk. The recreation yard two floors below us was a ghost town. Even the schizophrenic students lacked the usual vigor in their back-and-forth rocking. Everything was quiet, almost as if they were waiting for something to happen.

And then something did happen.

One of my students asked, "Why don't we sing a Christmas song?"

"Let's sing 'Rudolph the Red-Nosed Reindeer!'" exclaimed another student.

Then silence fell again. The students all stared at each other.

Finally another asked, "Who's gonna start?" Another silence.

One of the schizophrenics stopped rocking about, smiled broadly, and began to sing.

"Rudolph . . . dah reddd . . . noosed . . . reinnndeahh." He was completely tone deaf, but had made a valiant effort. I couldn't help it. I had to jump in and sing with him. Then everyone joined in, including those in their cells: the toilet flusher, the screamers, even Albert the giant. Everyone seemed to have a good time. Even some guards joined us for the third verse.

When class was over, I picked up my materials and wished all of them a Merry Christmas. As I turned to the security officer, he said, "That's one for the record books. I have never seen anything happen like that here." As I was leaving, my eight students were singing another round of Rudolph.

"Merry Christmas," I said quietly to the security officer.

"Merry Christmas, Mr. Humphries."

As I left the cellblock, I had a sinking feeling in my stomach. Unlike out in the free world, the holiday season brings depression to most of the incarcerated. I wondered, while our families shared in the Yuletide spirit, who among my students would fall victim to the beast within and take his own life?

Deer Hunt

For Elwood, deer, meaning the hunted kind, were a powerful symbol. The Ellis Unit had been a fearful place for him. He became convinced someone was going to kill him if he stayed at Ellis too long. Because he thought no one believed him, he started slashing his arms with a contraband razor, not with the intent of ending his life but so officials would send him to the treatment center for observation.

Elwood was in his early thirties, soft-spoken and very withdrawn. I taught him only twice and in every picture he drew a single deer, presumably a symbol of himself.

I remember I asked him, "Why do you draw deer?"

"Because you never stop running for your life."

He was sent back to Ellis after two weeks with us. One day he slashed too deep and bled to death at the Ellis Unit. Once again, the beast had dragged another victim to its lair.

Return to Sender

His name was David. Because our treatment center couldn't adequately administer the psychiatric care he needed, they convinced Rusk State Hospital to take him. After a few weeks, Rusk sent him back. This inmate had been too much, even for the staff at Rusk.

At least they sent him properly gift-wrapped. We received him bound to a stretcher with heavy leather straps, wearing a straitjacket and iron shackles on his ankles. Only his head was free to move. Decades later, Hollywood would give the world a picture of what I mean, with Anthony Hopkins, starring as Hannibal Lecter in *Silence of the Lambs*, wheeled out on a stretcher, bound and masked: Except we didn't have the mask yet.

I happened to be heading back to my office for a cup of coffee when I saw a group of correctional officers rolling David into the run between A and B block. They placed him, still bound to the stretcher, on the concrete floor, and then stood far away from him, looking tense. I had never seen a man bound like an animal, so the sight made my skin crawl.

But none of this seemed to faze the head guard, Major Herriage. He just marched right up to the inmate, fearless and unusually chipper.

"I hear you weren't too happy with your stay at Rusk. They're saying you were a challenge to their 'professional integrity.' Kept making life hard on the nurses. They said you'd be more comfortable with us here at Walls. Not that I like the idea, so I'll suppose we now have the honor of making you feel right at home." This got a nervous chuckle from the guards.

"See? The boys here are ready to give you a king's welcome! But I do have to ask you one question: Are you going to behave so we can put you in your house? Because there are two ways we can handle this: the easy way or the hard way."

For a moment, David just stared at the ceiling. An eerie silence hung in the air, when suddenly the inmate lurched toward the Major Herriage and began biting at his boots with powerful thrusts of his body.

"Hey now, these are my newest pair of boots," hissed the Major. "I guess it's going to be the hard way! Sedate him!"

It took about six guards and a medical technician to carry out the order. I swallowed hard as I realized he would be in my class, sans shackles and straitjacket.

David's arms and neck were covered with layers of deep, self-inflicted slash wounds. But he wasn't the hunted deer. No, he was far from Elwood, the soft-mannered man who met an untimely death shortly after returning to Ellis. This inmate was only allowed to attend my class under heavy sedation. He was muscular, partially bald, and looked to be about thirty-five. His face remained expressionless, with eyes that looked through me—the kind of look that Golda Rich warned me about after the Carrasco siege.

As we stood over David's now-limp body, the guards cautioned me about his penchant for sudden acts of great violence. They said he had a deep, primeval urge to destroy any living thing, no matter the injury to himself.

"His victims suffered severe overkill, and when I—" the same guard who told the Frankenstein story started to say.

"That'll be enough, sir!" I interrupted. Just the thought of the last overkill story he told me sent chills down my spine.

And I really did feel a chill at that moment, though it was more physical than psychological. As we stood there, watching the guards wheel him off to solitary where he would wait until the appropriate housing measures could be met, a cool breeze snaked around my body. It slithered from me to the group of guards and medics. Coats were clutched close and blazers were buttoned. That first cool draft always put me off. So many months spent acclimating to sweating in my dress shirts, and now right when I got comfortable with the humidity, the weather changed. Just as it had been obscenely hot inside our schoolhouse yet temperate inside the cellblock, our classes were becoming comfortably cool. Meanwhile all the cellblocks sank deeper into a rigid, constant cold.

Naked Suicide

Billy did not produce many drawings. But then one afternoon he traced his hands in the overlapping image I had seen before. Reginald, the student who had drawn the Rolls Royce, had drawn the same symbol before his untimely suicide. This time I knew what to expect and notified the clinical staff that Billy was a suicide risk.

"We are aware of his suicidal tendencies," droned a nonchalant nurse I'd never seen before. "We monitor all of our patients daily. There isn't much an art teacher like you can do to help us."

"Dr. White and Mr. Habib are both aware of this as an indicator of an imminent inmate suicide," I retorted in my most convincing, drill sergeant tone. "This drawing has been seen before, shortly before another inmate killed himself. Now it is here again, in a completely unrelated instance. I suggest you take this information to your superiors; or I should call Dr. White at his home on his day off?"

"No, no, that won't be necessary." That seemed to have gotten his attention. "I can see to it he is put in a strip cell this afternoon."

It was Tuesday and I wouldn't be back at the treatment center until Thursday, but it didn't matter. Billy was dead by then. As I drove home down a rain-drenched FM 247, I wondered if the nurse would make good on his promise. A storm front brought another cold and nasty two days to Huntsville. The cellblocks would have been unbearably cold.

Thursday, I was back and enjoying my lunch in the officers dining hall. The same technician from Tuesday was also there. Since he had no company, I sidled up and joined him.

"Hello there. I think we got off on the wrong foot. I'm Jim Humphries. You should know the research we're doing here at Walls is quite new to the field of psychoanalysis."

"Yes, I'm aware of the program and of who you are," he replied blithely. This time he didn't even make eye contact with me. If there is one thing I can't stand, it's when a man won't look you in the eye when he talks to you!

But then he did look up at me and said bluntly, "The inmate who drew the symbol of his overlapping hands is dead."

"What?" I choked out. "When did this happen?"

"Last night," he droned. "Somehow, he procured a pencil and used it to stab himself in the stomach. So we took him to the prison hospital with strict instructions to keep him in a strip cell, with no clothes at all. But last night they had only an inmate worker available to watch over him."

"For Christ's sake! The inmates don't give a damn about each other!" I was beside myself but the nurse just continued relating his story in the same tone of indifference.

"The patient was moaning and calling out for something to keep him warm. The inmate worker told us his moans and cries were wearing down his patience, so he threw a white jumpsuit into the cell and told him to shut up. A half hour later, the patient was found hanging naked from the cell door. The jumpsuit legs were tied to the top of the cell door, with his head in the crotch. He used his own body weight to hang himself from his neck, cutting off circulation to his brain. He was dead before any hospital personnel were able to get to him."

I sighed heavily.

"Hey, you were right about him. He would've died on my watch, but because of you I don't have to fill out half a day's paperwork."

In my experience with suicides, shortly before they take their own life, they appear to be in full control. They fool mostly everyone into thinking they are rational and not depressed. In fact, they usually appear quite calm, by then having reached a resolve about themselves and the world.

Billy had devised a plan to circumvent the precautions of the treatment center. He knew that as long as he was in the treatment cellblock, he would be watched too closely. So by stabbing himself, he was moved to where he could take advantage of an impatient inmate worker and trick him into providing the means to take his own life. Soon he'd only be remembered around the treatment center as a statistic for prison suicide. But as for me, I never forgot him.

To the doctors, they were just patients; just inmates to the prison guards; and convicts to society. To me, though, they were all my students and each one's death caused me grief. Though I had barely known Billy, his death reminded me of how fragile life can be.

Volleyball Backup

The security officer pointed out to me an inmate doing multiple sit-ups in the run in front of A-Block. Kenneth was a middle-aged, red-headed man, medium height and build, with his right hand bandaged up. *He's not a typical patient for art therapy, so why is he here in my class?* I thought.

Before I came any closer, I decided to check his file: "Former contract killer for the Southern mafia . . . prone to extreme acts of violence if provoked . . . psychologically stable . . . observation patient only," it read. Since he seemed to have the habit of hurting or killing other inmates, the only place suitable to house him was the Walls Treatment Center while the facts of his involvement in an incident were sorted out. This was good news to me: At least this guy wouldn't drool on the artwork.

He glanced up at me from the floor and seemed to notice the file under my arm but kept on with his sit-ups. I approached, letting the heels of my cowboy boots thud with every step. He paused again.

"So, you're the art teacher I've heard about?"

"Yes. When you're finished, join us in class."

"Okay," he grunted.

He attended my class several times at the treatment center, usually due to his involvement in an incident that needed investigation. As for me, I had no reason to judge him harshly. We even became friendly. We were both former Marines, so right off we shared an unspoken camaraderie. We also had some other things in common, though his story was more colorful than my own.

While serving with the Marines, he had the opportunity to fight as a middleweight boxer representing his Marine unit. I'd been the regional Golden Gloves champion for Canton, Mississippi, before I enlisted. He was a former student of the same school district I had worked for. He became a varsity fullback, garnering the attention of University of Texas scouts. But this dream was short-lived: He was kicked off the team when the school enforced a new policy: no married students would be allowed to represent the school in any athletic competition. Crushed by this cruel twist of fate, he dropped out and joined the Marines.

Word of our friendship reached our E&R man, who was formerly the captain in charge of death row at Ellis Unit. He called me into his office and informed me of this inmate's homicidal past and tendency to occasionally kill inmates while in prison.

"I understand you've been talking a lot with him. Rumor has it you may even be on friendly terms."

"Yes," I replied. "In accordance with my efforts to put my students at ease, by answering whatever reasonable questions they might ask me, and answering questions that are not personal or inappropriate."

I was always on my guard with our E&R man. He seemed to speak to teachers in the same manner he spoke to convicts, even sometimes with less respect. He was proud of his time at Ellis and made it clear to everyone that he considered having been a death row captain a badge of honor. Leaning back in his seat, the E&R man slowly rotated a pencil between his fingers, scowling back at me.

"You should know he's talked more with you than he ever did with me when he was on death row. In fact, treatment personnel inform me he has talked more with you than with anyone, ever!"

"Well, he feels comfortable in my class. So if a student wants to express themselves to feel better, why not?"

"Hmmph," he snorted. "And that's another reason why I can't stand you Windham folk, always talking about these men like they're children at your school. Mr. Humphries, these men are bad men. Some of them are vicious killers, and Kenneth is no exception. All I'm saying is be careful. It wouldn't be wise to get too friendly."

"I appreciate the warning, sir."

I thought of myself as a good judge of a man's character and something about what the E&R man said didn't sit well with me. I knew the men in prison had all done some sort of wrong, but there is more to a man's nature than his actions. Could Kenneth be just that, a true deviant with just another good story? I turned over this problem in my head hundreds of times. I was again losing sleep, so one day while in class, I had to ask.

During one session, Kenneth came up to me deep in thought. He was trying to find the right color for a tree line in his painting. I told him to use autumn colors like orange and yellow, because it was October.

"Thank you," he said, leaving for his seat.

"What kind of trouble do you get into that they send you here?"

My question stopped him in mid-step.

"What did you say?" He turned to look at me with that stone cold stare again.

"I've had you in my class for over three years now, but you're not like these other guys. So why are you, of all places, here at the treatment center?"

"Usually it happens because some convict thinks that he can get the best of me. Sometimes it's a row tender who thinks that he can handle me." He relaxed his glare and stepped closer to recall a story about an inmate who had tried to kill him.

"He thought a three-inch shank would be enough. Ha! I've been stabbed by knives twice as long and lived. So there I was, going through my daily sit-ups, when out of the blue I feel a pinch on my neck. I reach back just as he stabs my hand straight through."

He showed me a scar on his palm.

"But that just pissed me off. So I take his little knife out of my hand, wrestle him to the ground, and saw his head off. When I was done, I threw his head down the run. It was a good thing, because that was when I was sent here and met you."

"That's one way of looking at it," I swallowed hard as I digested the story.

"A man's got to have a code of honor, Mr. Humphries," he continued. "In my line of work, I've seen real vicious killers who had no respect for human life. Not me, no. I live by two simple rules: I don't hurt women or their children, and no man will ever cross me. Guess that's why I'm always winding up in here with you. These men are always trying to cross me."

"Shot in the cross . . ." I mumbled.

"Come again?"

"Ah, nothing. Just a little lesson I've learned here at TDC. I agree with you that these men are always a little shifty."

"Ha!" Kenneth flung his head back laughing. "Shifty! Funny man, Mr. Humphries."

My principal asked me if I could expand my program at the treatment center to include a physical education (PE) program. Now, teaching in a classroom is one thing, but conducting a PE class in the prison yard, where the nearest guard is far above in a guard tower, is another. However, with my second child on the way, I needed all the additional hours I could get. So I figured the best approach was to supervise their exercise program.

On the first day of PE, I was to go down to the yard and play volleyball with some of the patients. On my way there, Kenneth came up to me and said, "Mr. Humphries, just so you know, when we go down there, I've got your back."

"Um, sure," I hesitated. "But I don't think that'll be necessary."

"Mr. Humphries, let me tell you something." He had that stone cold stare again. "You're no phony. You're for real and I want you to stay that way. So as long as I am here, I want to help you. You should know that the guards observe the patients from the run three stories up, not down where you will be."

"Take a look at those guys, Mr. Humphries," he continued. "Most of those men are not your students. No, no. You get the pick of the litter for your classes, the 'most sane' of the bunch. But when we're down in the yard, they'll all be there, every slobbering and moaning dimwit we have here. Hell, it's like the *Night of the Living Dead* down there!"

And he was right. One loose cannon off his meds with me in the middle of the hornet's nest didn't inspire much confidence. Kenneth was also very resourceful. Since he had been incarcerated, he had his death sentence commuted to life while earning an associate degree. He wasn't crazy, just ice cold to anyone who meant him any harm. I appreciated his insight and accepted his protection.

The first day we played volleyball was . . . interesting. As agreed, Kenneth played the position behind me. Inmate patients who were unable to make sense of volleyball shuffled around the perimeter of the exercise area. Just a few feet separated us from a ring of men whose sanity hung by a thread. I tried to not think about it as the game went on. When I looked back at this steely hit man, I saw him standing fast and unnerved among a sea of white uniforms. This was truly his element.

Luckily, I never had any problems. But one day in my absence, all hell broke loose. The whole hospital was abuzz with excitement when I returned.

"So this new patient was on the yard for the first time," a guard told me. "He's a first-time felon, so you know he's young and stupid. Without warning, he takes off running! He hits the wire fence around the yard, clawing his way up, real fast. But then right behind him, your hit man comes running after him. Now both of them are on the fence heading toward the roof, but Kenneth catches up before they get to the top."

"How high were they?" I asked.

"Oh, just about three stories up! Yeah, that kid sure can climb. He was up on a service pipe by the time Kenneth got to him and hooked him around the waist, saying 'Your choice! We both taste concrete or we go down to the top of the run. It doesn't make any difference to me!' Ha! So the kid looks down, scared shitless, and then just freezes there on the pipe. So the hit man yanks him down and drags him to the service door on the top of the run. When we pulled the kid back inside, he looked happier to be with us than with the other guy! Meanwhile, the hit man just stood there on the top of the run, acting all hot shit, with the whole yard cheering. So we let him soak in his glory. Gotta say, he deserved it."

The next day an ample amount of concertina wire was strung across the wire fence enclosure, immediately below the run, to prevent any more attempts at jackrabbit escapes. The young inmate had intended to make it to the roof of Five Building, run west, jump the wall, and drop down thirty feet to freedom. Certain death would have awaited him had he made it that far, because a heavily armed guard was picketed there, ready to shoot any escapee on sight.

Shortly after that, my principal called me and said the administration decided to hire a full-time teacher for the treatment center who was certified in special education. He thanked me for my help in pioneering the education program, and to my surprise, asked me if I had any recommendations for my replacement.

"Yes, I have just one. Be sure he's a military veteran."

And so they did, hiring an excellent teacher, one who had served with the U.S. Navy. He had a friendly, easy-going attitude, but he didn't take any bullshit from anyone, not even our E&R man.

I continued my art therapy work, but still took a little time now and again to catch up with Kenneth whenever they brought him in for another round of "observation." He always had some wild story to tell, which usually ended in him maiming some foolish inmate.

Burnout

Not all of my schizophrenic students had been diagnosed as needing psychiatric help. I had one inmate student in my regular day class who really had a problem with women. Now, usually I allowed a student to draw whatever came to his mind. Until a student realized he needed help, there was no constructive reason to impose it, so I just let the patients draw to the limits of their sanity.

Harry was of medium height, with dark hair and a vacant, faraway stare in his eyes. Everything about him was unassuming, so nothing could have prepared me for what happened when his crayon touched paper. He only used two colors, red and black. His drawings needed none other, for he only drew distorted images of women that were twisted, broken, or chopped up in terrible and bloody ways. I had seen drawings like his many times before, but for only a short time and only by some of the worst criminally insane inmates at the center. But this inmate was just another inmate in the regular population. Day in and day out, he continued to draw his gut-wrenching material, never once asking for help or saying anything at all.

Occasionally I tried to encourage him to share with me the meaning behind his drawings. I had this futile hope that I could help him to reach beyond himself for inspiration, instead of turning inward to create such crude and disgusting pictures. Alas, I was unable to get through to him. The beast had swallowed his soul, allowing chaos and destruction to spill out onto the paper. All that remained was an empty shell, barren and rotted. Just standing close to him made me feel as though every bit of my joy were being slowly siphoned away.

Then one evening I was watching *Lifeline*, a television show that aired actual footage, not reenactments, of real trauma cases from hospital emergency rooms. The program's field reporter, Napoleon Johnson, related an incident where several women had been viciously attacked. The television crew followed the medical staff of Herman Hospital, in Houston, into a treatment room where some of the victims were being treated. They appeared so mangled, bruised, or broken, they hardly resembled human beings. The doctors spoke in a detached medical jargon, talking about what they were doing to "save these women's lives," never once wincing at their horrid injuries. Then we were shown the assailant who had been captured at the scene—a white man with dark hair and a vacant stare. There on the TV screen, in my own home, was the mug shot of my student. He hadn't been drawing figments from his imagination. He'd been drawing his memories! Memories of heinous acts of violence against innocent women he lived out every day, in my class!

I almost instantly lost my equilibrium and the room started to spin. All I could hear was the pounding of my heartbeat in

my head. I fell off the couch and came close to vomiting. I switched off the television and lay on my back, waiting for my stomach to settle down. There I stayed, wondering about all the evils of the world and how my work brought me closer to these evils than ever before. *How could anyone want to recreate such behavior again and again in drawings? And why hadn't he been committed to the treatment center?* Then I remembered the criteria for being committed: The inmate had to be a danger to himself and dysfunctional in the regular prison population. Function, he could. Pose a danger to other inmates, all of whom were male? Not likely, at least as far as the administration was concerned.

The next day I inquired as to what kind of sentence Harry had received. I was shocked to learn only twenty years. And his case was on appeal, too! Anger and frustration with our legal system and the results coming out from our courts began to weigh heavily on my mind. Perhaps I had worked for the prison system too long. Seeing the victims of one of my students turned me off from wanting to help all of my inmate students. A sense of disgust clouded my judgment. I asked myself, *"Why am I here? Is this what I've become, an oblivious art teacher to the killers of the world?"*

I was drowning in a vortex of despair when Celeste, my wife, reached down and lifted me back to life with the keen wisdom I had fallen in love with: "Jim, you need to get away from there. It's eating you up inside." The next morning, I walked into Principal Chris Tracy's office to submit my resignation.

"What's the matter, Jim?" Chris asked. "You don't look so well."

"I'm not, Mr. Tracy."

"Sit down then. Let me get you something. Have you had your coffee yet?"

"No, not yet but—"

"Just hold tight. I don't want you skipping out on me, okay?"

He scurried off to the teacher's lounge and returned with two hot cups of Folgers Instant, made just the way I like it, with a bit of sugar and a drop of milk. I felt my cheeks turned red as I sipped the morning brew, and for a moment I could forget everything. Mr. Tracy snapped me back to reality.

"So Jim, now that I've brought some color back to your face, what can I do you for?"

"Chris, I've had the worst week," I sighed. "I saw this *Lifeline* show on TV, and since then, it feels like my world just fell apart. I can't be the teacher I once was."

Mr. Tracy's grin vanished from his face. He put his coffee mug down, leaned back in his chair and stared at the ceiling for a while. I didn't know what to do, so I just sat there waiting for him to respond.

"I know the show you're talking about. Likes to make a fuss and air actual footage of crime scenes. Makes me sick to my stomach every time I catch my wife watching it, but she likes to know what kind of men I work with."

He sat up, slurped some coffee down, and then leaned forward on his elbows, peering at me through the steam of his mug.

"I know he's one of ours, too. I'd know those spacey eyes any time of day." He paused to take a deep breath. "I had hoped you didn't see that last episode. Already I've had another teacher request that he be removed from her class. Now, are you here to give me that same song and dance?"

"Yes, err, I mean no." Now I had to pause and gather my wits. "It's just that I've been seeing for weeks now what goes on in his head."

"What do you mean, Jim?"

"He draws pictures of mutilated women. Nothing else: just women being tortured or cut to pieces."

His eyes widened in disbelief. "I had no idea! That's horrible." Then he added, "But you have to know we got some real monsters here, Jim."

"I know that, Chris. Remember, I've worked in the treatment center."

"Right, right, you did." Another silence settled in, but I couldn't bear to stall any more. I had to break the news of my resignation to him.

"Chris, I just can't anymore. I'm burned out on teaching inmates."

"So, you're resigning?"

I had agreed to work a twelve-month contract when I returned from Austin back in 1974. It was now 1979, and the five years had taken a toll on me. We, including my inmate artists, Windham, and TDC in general, had accomplished a lot with the program I'd developed. But now none of that seemed to matter. The beast was winning this one, and I could do nothing to stop it. It had devoured those women, had drained a man of his soul, and now it was eating away at mine.

"Yes, Chris. I have to resign before I do or say something I'll regret." Mr. Tracy looked mildly displeased, then shrugged and leaned back in his chair.

"Well, I'm not going to try to change a man's mind when he's made it up."

And so he accepted my resignation. Mr. Tracy knew very well that TDC workers suffered from burnout and sympathized with me. He did me a further favor by calling a fellow principal at Conroe High School on my behalf. A week later I was teaching science at Conroe High. My time away from TDC enabled me to gain a new perspective in teaching inmates. To say I missed my inmate students would be a stretch. Nevertheless, they were just more interesting to teach than teenagers. So, believe it or not, at the end of the school year, I went back to Ellis to teach math. By then I felt spiritually refreshed and ready to take on the assignment of teaching felony offenders.

Anyone who works in the field of corrections must first keep the beast at bay in their own life, before they can face the beast in the lives of others.

RETURN 7 TO ELLIS

New Beginnings

THE ELLIS UNIT IS THE kind of classic, hard-time prison you've seen in movies, complete with a death row block. Even with the reputation of its hardened criminal population, most Texans are unaware of the unique industries that operate there. For example, all school buses in the state of Texas were refurbished at Ellis. Occasionally, an old fire truck would need a good once-over, a job that never ceased to delight the inmate mechanics. A major portion of the wooden desks for public school teachers and state offices was built there. Government-issued shoes, work boots and clothing were manufactured at Ellis as well. Sometimes the very shoes a guard wore were sewn by the inmates he supervised.

In addition to the prison industry, Ellis operated a large farm, which provided fresh meats, dairy products, and vegetables for the prison cafeteria. Oh boy, was it good! Eating a meal or taking a coffee break was always an adventure, but having the coffee station close to the dessert shelf was a recipe for dietary disaster. Coffee in the morning has always been essential to my routine, and those delicious snacks from our bakery needed to be devoured in concert with a hot cup of joe.

Most people like their pastries fresh, but for me they needed to be a little stiff in texture or downright hard. If I couldn't forcefully jab my fork into a piece of cake or biscuit, I didn't eat it. You might think I've had one too many pieces of mystery meat, so I'll explain.

On every table sat a small, metal pitcher of the freshest dairy cream. There were plenty of milk cows on the Ellis farm, so our cream came straight their udders. There are few gastronomic pleasures I enjoy outside of my wife's cooking, but eating stale cake soaked in Ellis cream was one of them. All I needed was a few minutes of idle conversation with a fellow staff member, while waiting for the cake to soak up the pure cream like a sponge.

Shortly after I returned to Ellis, my yearly physical indicated that I had not only gained weight but also had a cholesterol count that was much too high. My doctor called it my "happy fat," because of my happy marriage and fatherhood. Yet he made me painfully aware that "all that is delicious is not necessarily nutritious," and further suggested it would be better for me to save the calorie count for my wife's excellent cooking. I did my best to follow my doctor's orders, yet every once in a while I fell off the wagon. Sometimes, those little steel pitchers looked so lonely, sitting all by themselves on the tables, with nary a slice of cake or piece of pastry to accompany them. Yes, those were times I just couldn't resist. It was my own guilty pleasure, my little secret I've kept until this day.

There was one dish at Ellis that deserved its name—Dynamite Chicken—because it literally looked as if the chicken had been blown up by a charge of dynamite. Our huge food processor resembled a contraption from a sci-fi or James Bond film. Its large opening was straight out of *Soylent Green*, with knobs and levers to adjust its processing power. This is where whole chickens met their final demise, to be violently mangled into chunks of raw fowl. The weird angles and large chunks produced pieces not normally served together, such as a wing with a chunk of backbone. Although the chicken did make for a dynamite meal, it took a little getting used to.

I returned to Ellis to find that the school hadn't changed at all. Ben Small was still the principal. The classrooms were still stiflingly hot, without any air-conditioning. I was there to teach math, though it wasn't the challenge I preferred. I really wanted to start an art program, yet the security department had an extremely guarded attitude toward all inmates and possibly considered art classes to be an unimportant a waste of time. It would be a hard sell, but apparently I had friends in high places because, a few months later, an old colleague paid me a visit.

"I heard the rumors but had to see it for myself! How the hell have you been?" I turned at the sound of the voice and there, at my classroom door, stood Chris Tracy, the same man I quit on back at Walls, beaming a smile at me and looking just as jolly as ever.

"I've been good, Chris," I replied. "Real good. Got two boys now, growing up strong."

"That's good to hear." He then peered at me the same way he did the day I resigned. "Hey, you never got back to me about that Conroe job."

"I'm sorry about that," I said sheepishly. "I needed a break from everything TDC. Nothing personal."

"Why are you back here then? Didn't it work out all right?"

"Oh, yeah, no problems. I really have to thank you for setting that up for me, but after a year of hormonal teenagers, I started to miss y'all. So I came back." I took a look around at my inmate students. "Hell Chris, I even missed these knuckleheads!" A few of my students smiled.

"Well, it's good to have you back. But why are you teaching math? You're the 'Windham Rembrandt': You should be teaching these men how to paint, not count."

Well, apparently I'd been given a nickname, and you know what? I kind of liked it.

"Thanks for noticing that. It's been nearly impossible to even suggest we start an art program here. Security isn't willing to consider it."

"They aren't, are they?" He raised an eyebrow, snickering. "Well, I'll have you know I'm now the assistant superintendent. Let me put in a good word and we'll see to it you're back in the art room."

Looking around at my sullen students, he added, "That is, if you want to."

"Oh, yes sir!"

"I'm glad you're on board!" Chris turned to leave but had to add one more thing. "Just don't do me like you did back at Walls." He left before I could tell him I wouldn't.

Prison Pigeons

For my return to the Ellis Unit, I was given a classroom at the end of our L-shaped school layout. It was small, hot and without a sink for water disposal. A decorative concrete block screen blocked out most the natural light. But that was the least of my worries: The major problem was that almost every window was full of bird shit, donated daily by prison pigeons roosting behind the concrete screen.

I pleaded with the facilities manager to have the droppings cleaned up but it never happened. They would remain a permanent element of our environment. Until we had a window A/C installed, there was only a window for ventilation. That meant the smell of prison pigeon poo wafted in as well.

99 Art Assistant

Several inmates applied for the position of art assistant, but only Joe stood out from the rest. It might be hard to believe, but I chose him because he was honest and cheerful. He also had an excellent talent

for landscape and wild-
life painting. Before join-
ing my class, he could be
found repairing the sew-
ing machines in the prison
garment factory, so he was
more pleased than I was
when he got the news of
his new assignment. But
when security was notified
of my choice, the death
row Captain Bogardus
called me in.

"Mr. Humphries,
I reckon?" the captain
greeted me. He was quite
a sight. Years of stress had
worn his face down to a
jagged concrete visage.
Dark circles cradled his eyes, eyes that glowered at me from deep sockets,
but it was his voice that left the most profound impression. He spoke
with a timbre that siphoned every bit of joy from his listener, an unin-
tended consequence from a lifetime of working with the condemned.
If I had ever imagined a caricature of a death row jailer, it would have
to look like him. He truly was the Captain of the Condemned.

"Sit down, Mr. Humphries." He was a man of few words. "I was
informed you've decided your workload here was not manageable, and
have since hired an assistant, a Mr. Joseph Mason." I noticed a single
inmate's file, several inches thick, sitting in front of him on his desk.

"Yes, sir, that is true."

His blue-grey eyes narrowed: "Do you know who this inmate is?"

"Yes, yes I do. He was on death row when the federal government commuted his sentence to a 99." A life sentence with the indicator "99" meant life without the possibility of parole.

"Mr. Humphries, Mr. Mason has a very checkered past."

The captain continued in great detail about my assistant's past, to be assured I was fully aware of what he had done to deserve capital punishment. Normally laconic and terse during the other times we'd spoken, the captain rarely spent more than a moment explaining anything. This lengthy explanation meant he took this case seriously.

When he finished, he asked, "Now, are you sure about this?"

"Yes, Captain."

He pressed further, unconvinced. "But why him?"

"Joseph's a good artist," I answered firmly. "And he's assured me he's accepted his fate, and thus wants to do something constructive with his life."

The captain took a long, suspicious look at me. He didn't buy my story but there was nothing he could do about it. So he just sat back in his chair, closed the inmate's file, and invited me to leave.

I had a good feeling about the choice I had made, so I called Joe into my classroom and introduced him to his new role. But just as we were getting comfortable with one another, he looked very serious and said to me, "Mr. Humphries, I will do my best to help you but you must remember that I am a convict. And if push comes to shove and I am forced to choose sides, I'll choose to stand with the other convicts. Don't ever forget that."

"Joe, I appreciate your candor," I replied. "Now, let's get to work. There are some jugs of wastewater in need of disposing. See to it they're properly disposed of."

I never regretted my choice to take on Joe as my assistant. During our three years of working together, he served the education department faithfully and flourished as an artist. I was proud of his progress and glad to be a part of it.

Paranoid Philosophy

My art program was a whole new experience for the Ellis Unit. I never once got the impression that the security personnel were convinced that my program was the least bit meritorious. By this time, I'd taught loonies at Huntsville, first-timers at Ferguson, and even some death row students and understood how things worked around here. For example, it didn't take long for the inmates to learn I accounted for every item of art supplies before they left my class. Twice an inmate tried to put a roll of masking tape in his socks, and twice I fouled his plan to smuggle his contraband.

Yet I still sensed something was not quite right where the attitude of the guards was concerned.

One morning I was feeling somewhat down. The guards had been making a fuss about my class, and this put my job in jeopardy. I didn't want to give in to pressure created by the rumors but for some reason I couldn't help it. I'd given too much to this program to lose it now.

"I must be getting paranoid," I muttered under my breath while passing the principal's office. I had not intended anyone to hear me, but alas, Zeke, the inmate bookkeeper, was sitting at his desk, looking me straight in the eye. All six-foot-five, two hundred thirty pounds of him got up from his typewriter and walked over to me. His forearms were inked with tattoos of several typical symbols used by the Aryan Brotherhood, such as the Nazi swastika and Iron Cross. I just stood there, not knowing what to do.

He loomed over me for a moment as he said, "Mr. Humphries, you're not paranoid. Your enemies are real." For some reason, that made me feel better.

Death Row Artist

October came and, with it, every Sunday came the Texas Prison Rodeo, the wildest, roughest, toughest rodeo in all of America's prisons. It was a special time for the inmates where they could feel proud of their units, compete against the guards in bull and buck riding events, or earn a little cash from the art sale. That's where you'd find me every year, organizing the displays and keeping the works in good order. Word of my students' work had been spreading over the Southwest for a number of years. Patrons knew quality when they saw it, and they came from as far away as Las Vegas just to snag, for instance, a high-quality desert landscape.

For reasons unknown to me, a death row inmate convinced Mr. Estelle, the director of the TDC, to order me to assist this inmate with his artwork. I reckon since most of the inmates who were well behaved, could take an art class and sell their works at our rodeo. His lawyers made a case that he was being unusually punished by

barring him from pursuing his artistic talents as well. That is, if he had any talent at all.

My first visit to the death row cell of Billy Hughes was a very surrealistic experience. Here the upper runs were enclosed by heavy gauge steel wire, to prevent jumpers from committing suicide. Rows of wall-mounted televisions provided the only entertainment allowed, together with an occasional outside visitor. As I was escorted to the inmate's cell, hands popped out of the cells in front and behind me. Each hand held a small mirror and through it, the inmates could see you and you them.

Suddenly the sound of hooting and hollering filled the cellblock. I looked at the guard, who appeared unconcerned. "Must be something on the TV," he said. I looked up at the TV to see a daytime soap opera, broadcasting a scene where an armed robber was attacking a woman in her kitchen. And whom did you think the inmates were cheering for? The robber, of course!

The guard introduced me to Billy. He seemed very relieved to see me. He gave me a list of some mounting and matting material that he needed and showed me some of his pen and ink illustrations of horses. They were actually pretty good and I understood why Mr. Estelle wanted him to sell his work at our Rodeo Art Show.

Many inmates helped out their families in the free world by sending home money they'd earned from their art sales. One afternoon while I was visiting Billy to pick up some more artwork, he started talking about the night he killed a highway patrolman. I had no idea why he wanted to talk to me, but I obliged him and listened to his story.

"After the cop stopped me, I got real scared. Man, I feared for my life," Billy said. "I see him coming up behind my car. I don't know if it was the drugs but I lost it, grabbed my pistol, shot through the back window, and took off in my car as fast as I could."

"So, you shot a highway patrolman because you were . . . what, scared?" I shot back.

"Hey, I had no idea if I hit him or not," he answered, looking like a cat who just ate the canary. "I mean, I didn't mean to kill him, so I can't be guilty of murder. I was high, man! High on drugs and alcohol! That makes me innocent of murder because you know I wouldn't have done that if I were sober. The drugs made me do it!"

And he continued to maintain his innocence until he was executed by lethal injection on January 24, 2000, at 6:18 p.m. All it took was a little too much alcohol, drugs, and paranoia to destroy the lives of two men, a Texas Deputy Trooper named Mark Frederick and his murderer, Billy Hughes. It destroyed the life of a dedicated young trooper who was doing his job in upholding the laws of the state of Texas, and the life of an intelligent and talented young man, who sadly had little regard for human life or the law. Billy's behavior was a mirror image of the value system of a law-abiding society. His decision to disregard the law was on a deadly collision course with a man who had sworn to uphold it. For twenty-four years, as Billy paced the floor of his cell, the beast nibbled away on Billy's soul.

It was difficult for me to listen to the inmates rationalize their crimes. So many couldn't come to terms with the fact they had committed a crime. They didn't seem to grasp that just because they were high on drugs, alcohol, or both, they were not precluded from criminal responsibility. Many times I heard them say, "Oh, but if I'd been sober I would have never . . . " and so on. I heard this same excuse from many inmates, men who refused to accept responsibility for the pain and suffering they caused their victims and families. Sometimes the inability to accept the reality of their crime festered inside their conscience to the point where some did indeed lose their minds. Denial, shock, guilt: Whatever it was, some men couldn't handle their own beast and would eventually end up at the treatment center, or dead.

My wife, Celeste, once asked me, "Will you be sad when Billy Hughes is executed?"

"Yes," I answered. "I'll have tears for the man Billy could have been and tears for the man Mark Frederick could have been. Both were lost to us when Billy embraced his beast and tore that young trooper's life away from him."

Classroom Conflict

Some days just start off bad. Lately, the sky had been looking like rain, but the clouds failed to do anything except block out every bit of sunlight while the humidity stayed unbearably high. My guayabera shirt stuck to my chest, moist from the sweaty drive to work. When I entered my classroom I encountered the foulest stench. A putrid mix of farm animal manure and pigeon poo laid waste to my olfactory organs. I could barely breathe. If I opened my mouth, then I would taste the odor and maybe lose my breakfast. If I breathed through my nose, my sinuses would scream for mercy, causing my head to throb from an awful headache.

After a few moments, I felt faint. I stumbled out of the classroom, gasping for air. Something didn't seem right. Had the inmates played some joke on me and left buckets of manure under the desks? I held my breath, and peeked in through the door. No, no manure. Were the pigeons flocking by the window by the thousands? I walked around to the outside of the window where the birds deposited their daily droppings. Nope. No pigeons today.

It really didn't matter much anymore. The schoolhouse bell had rung, and the day's classes were to begin shortly. I took leave of my usual post at the front of the classroom and stood outside the door, watching the inmates file in and expecting someone to protest the smell. But as they took their seats, none of them winced or seemed to take any notice.

For about thirty minutes, all was well. Suddenly Lester, one of the younger African American students stood up from his stool and began to whoop and holler. His words were all strung together, in what seemed like an endless breath of air. All I could make out was he was mad. Probably at me . . . no . . . he was mad at white people. And since we're in the South . . . and since I was the whitest man in the room, he looked at as if I was the reason he went to prison. Well, at least it wasn't a personal attack.

I hadn't ever done Lester wrong, and he'd always been well behaved in class. *Maybe it was the pigeon poo getting to this brain?* I thought. Whatever it was, he was getting his second wind by now. The other inmates froze in place, except for a 1% biker-type named Bob who had eased quietly out the back of the room and out the door. *Hopefully he's going to get help*, I thought. Lester, meanwhile, remained where he was, and now that he was all warmed up, he let loose another volley of racial accusations and vulgarities.

I decided the best thing to do was relax and wait for him to talk himself out. I thought a display of some strong body language might help, so I sat down at the large gray steel table, took off my glasses, and placed them in the desk drawer. And for first time since my employment with TDC, I sized up an inmate. Lester and I were about the same weight and height, but his arms were longer. My time as a sergeant tank commander in the 49th Armored Division of the Texas Army National Guard kept me in good physical shape, but I would also need to use my boxing and other military experience if things got violent.

Finally, Lester seemed to be running out of steam. The endless tirade of absurd accusations trailed off as he took a look around him at the other students. Expressionless, they paid him little attention. The 1% biker came back in and casually took his seat in the back of the room. I thought he had run off to get help but no had guard followed him in. Before my hotheaded student could regain his momentum, I casually raised my hand to ask for my chance to speak. Lester looked puzzled for a moment and looked around again, as if expecting someone to back him up. No one had paid him any notice, not even the other African American inmates. It was as if he wasn't even there.

"Let's take a smoke break," I announced to the whole class, sounding more drill sergeant than art teacher. Everyone filed out calmly. Lester, who had just minutes before wanted me to "burn in hell," was waiting for me by the door. Gone was the anger and hatred. He just stood there, looking all dejected and sheepish, unable to make eye contact.

"Mr. Humphries, I'm really sorry 'bout that," he began. Without a word, I beckoned him to walk by my side as the class walked down the hall.

"I saw *Roots* on TV last night," he continued. "It tore me up, Mr. Humphries! Seeing my people treated like dogs, then getting up this morning in no better a place than those slaves! I just had to go off on some white man! Sorry that had to be you."

"Relax. I understand." I told him that my family had lived in the South for generations, but never had the resources to own land or slaves. I told him about Major General Patrick Cleburne's radical proposal to General Bragg and President Jefferson Davis to free all the slaves and arm them in the battle against the Union. He was bewildered to think there were black soldiers in the Confederate Army, fighting the Union during the Civil War. I recommended he check out some history books from the prison library, and then quickly changed the subject.

I left the inmate with the other students, so I could steal away to the principal's office for a quick cup of coffee. There, I found Zeke, the giant inmate bookkeeper lurking in the doorway, looking anxious. He moved out of the way to let me in, but closed in and followed me to the coffee pot. Now I was getting nervous, trying my best to look natural as I searched for the sugar and creamer.

"That inmate who left your classroom came in here and asked me for a shank," Zeke said. "He said someone was in Mr. Humphries's face. But I told him you could handle it."

I stopped pouring the creamer and looked up at him.

"Plus, killing that man would add five more years to his sentence. He's a friend of mine and I just couldn't let him do that with his parole hearing next year."

I glanced at the Nazi swastika and skull tattooed on his forearm, pondered the uncomfortable irony of the moment, then looked up and said, "Thank you."

The Murder of Warden Pack

One afternoon in late March 1981, the sun was hanging low above the horizon as I left Ellis to begin the trek home. As I walked down the front sidewalk, I noticed someone standing beside a car parked in the warden's space. Word had it that a man named Wallace M. Pack was going to be our new warden. I had never seen that car parked there before, and no one dared to take that spot, even when the warden was on vacation, so I presumed the stranger must have been this new warden.

The man was tall, slender, and wearing a traditional western-style hat that seemed to be standard issue for high-ranked officials in the TDC. I tried to get a good look at Warden Pack's face, but all I saw was a shadowed blur. I took off my glasses, cleaned them on my *guayabera,* and took another look. I could see the details of his coat, shirt, and tie but his face remained a blurred silhouette. This felt weird because another prison official was right there conversing with him, and I could see his face perfectly. During the drive home, I turned the situation over and over in my head. "C'mon Jim," I said aloud to myself. "You're not that old. The sun was just playing a trick on your eyes."

The next time I saw Warden Pack was at his funeral. Not long after that strange sighting, on April 4, 1981, he and Farm Manager Billy Max Moore were murdered by an inmate named Elroy Brown. A few days after their deaths, I talked with one of the correctional officers who had helped in the inmate's capture.

"Was it difficult for you to bring Brown back alive?" I asked him.

"No," the officer answered bluntly. "We wanted to bring him in and do it the right way."

Everyone assumed it would be an open-and-shut case of capital murder, with a quick trial and a death sentence. However, after a trial in Huntsville and a second one in Galveston, two different juries failed to convict Elroy Brown of murder. His lawyer had argued a successful case for self-defense by putting the character of the deceased Warden on trial. Pack's family, friends, colleagues, as well as most of the TDC personnel, including me, were profoundly disappointed with the trial's results. Many of us felt our justice system had failed.

The news of the verdict shocked everyone except my inmate students. In fact, my class seemed especially cheerful on the day of Brown's acquittal. Even my assistant had an extra bounce in his step. I don't know if it was their collective cheerfulness that made me uncomfortable, but something didn't sit right with me. At the time I had no knowledge of Warden Pack's history prior to Ellis, but apparently they knew something I didn't.

As it turned out they did, and so did investigative journalist William P. Barrett, who at the time was the Houston Bureau Chief for the Dallas Times Herald. In the April 12th and 15th, Mr. Barrett wrote two articles for the Herald that reported on the details of the Brown trial. Barrett reported that Wallace Pack had been accused of brutality by the inmates at the TDC Wynne Unit, near Huntsville, on numerous occasions. Pack had even been put on trial in 1978. At this trial, testimony revealed that while a warden at Wynne, he had a policy of intimidating writ-writers, the inmates who help their fellow convicts file formal complaints against prison officials.

Barrett also reported that during the same 1978 trial, Billy Max Moore was questioned about the death of an inmate named James Batts in 1977. Numerous inmates testified that they witnessed Batts being severely beaten by guards as he was moved into a truck driven by Moore, but Moore claimed he didn't see the incident. Even one of Pack's own prison guards, James Eckles Jr., testified on behalf of the inmates. His testimony detailed how Pack had given him and other guards special orders on how to treat the writ writers. The 1978 trial was a culmination of tens of thousands of pages from lawsuits filed against Pack and his colleagues, during the same decade where riots at Attica brought to the public's attention the issues of inmate treatment and the brutality of outdated methods of execution. Nevertheless, Pack was not convicted.

I had no idea who Warden Pack was, nor did I ever meet him. Years later, after I found out about the trials prior to his murder, the story of his untimely death and the blurred face I'd seen that late afternoon began to make sense. It's a rare moment to witness that moment when a man's façade fades to reveal his true nature. Surely it is easy for the beast to hide in the broad daylight or behind the mask of trusted authority, but during that strange afternoon in the parking lot, during the magic hour of twilight where darkness and light dance together in harmony, perhaps what I glimpsed at was Warden Pack's face melting away for just a moment to reveal his own beast.

Man of Stone

I often wondered why the inmates wanted to take my art class. Some of them were very talented, exhibiting deftness and skill I'd had seen only at the university level. Others were just beginners who wanted to doodle for a couple of hours a week, and a few began as complete novices but then later flourished into extraordinary painters. The students could choose either to advance their knowledge of the acrylic media on canvas board or work with soft pastel on colored pastel paper.

You can spend a lifetime learning different techniques for each medium and never master either one. Maybe it was the freedom they felt while painting or drawing, because they told me art class was the only place that was free from the rigidity of prison life. There, each of them could escape the cold concrete walls and create worlds of warm canyons or blue oceans where their souls could drink in the sunshine. They could share succulent meals with family members, drive down never-ending highways, and enjoy the pristine beauty of an undisturbed pond on a summer's morning. All I had to do was guide them along the right path, and their imaginations would run wild. Most of my students told me that art class day was the highlight of their week.

One morning a very unusual African American student named Alex joined my class. Alex stood approximately six and a half feet tall and appeared to be very physically fit, but his close-cropped white hair and yellowing whites of his eyes hinted at his real age. His detached behavior gave the impression he was somewhere else. He rarely ever looked right at you but seemed to be gazing through you. He didn't have that cold, soul-siphoning glare I'd seen in mentally disturbed inmates, but a softer, almost temporal look.

He never spoke to anyone except me, and my inmate assistant Joe. And he never smiled. That was just his nature. Looking at his face, I wondered if he ever did smile. The rigid angles of his face and head appeared to have been carved from stone. The texture of his skin resembled freshly quarried black granite, jagged with wrinkles and withered by scars. I would have loved to sketch a portrait or sculpt a bust of him, though I kept that thought to myself.

One day as I escorted the class down the hall for our afternoon restroom and smoke break, I spoke with one of the students and

reminisced on the progress of our art program. Second-hand smoke hung motionless in the warm humid air as another Texas summer hammered down rays of heat outside. I surveyed my students: some of them had never been given a chance in their lives or even a word of encouragement. Some of them had abusive fathers, drug-addicted mothers, or no families at all. And despite the fact that most of these men had never seen the inside of a high-school classroom, they were all able to grasp complex methods of drawing and painting. I'd had students at Dobie High School who couldn't learn in a whole school year what some of these men could master in two months!

"It's too bad that so much talent is locked up here," I muttered to myself, unaware that anyone had overheard me.

A deep bass voice came from above and said, "This is the best place for them: either here or in the graveyard." I looked up at the stone-faced Alex as he stared straight ahead into infinity. Those were the most words I had heard him say. Looking at his expressionless, hard-set face, for a moment I imagined him as an African king from another era of history, looking at a distant horizon envisioning the future of his people.

A few days later I found myself facing a potentially explosive problem with two students that could have led to violence. It started with a tall slender blond white inmate, whom I'll call Jed. Jed wore a permanent scowl and had a teardrop tattooed at the corner of his left eye. I had learned to sense the mood of my students through the tone of their voices and body language. Jed had never revealed anything about himself in my class: any happiness, sense of humor, or even a desire to enjoy my class. But then on that day, he chose to start some serious trouble.

As tensions rose in the classroom, I realized the nearest guard was down the long L-shaped hallway outside. I told Joe, my assistant, I would go get help. Then, the second I stepped out of the classroom, stone-faced Alex jumped up and planted himself in the doorway, facing in, his huge arms outstretched to block the exit.

"Sit down!" he thundered. "None of you are going anywhere until Mr. Humphries returns!" Alex's booming voice echoed down the hallway, loud enough, apparently, to catch the attention of the guard who intercepted me halfway, looking concerned.

Moments later, I returned with the officer on duty. He looked up at Alex. I could see he was thinking about taking some sort of action, yet hesitating about it. "He's not our trouble maker," I told him. "That one is!" I pointed at the culprit.

The matter ended without further incident, thanks, I believe, to Alex's intervention.

As for Jed's attempt to cause trouble, I rarely experienced such problems during my thirteen years at Windham and among the men at the Ellis Unit. Most of my students during that time came to love every minute of my classes, a fact I appreciate always.

Once a man is incarcerated, the free world no longer exists to him. It becomes a dream of what could be and a memory of what was. The present no longer exists in free world terms. That's why it's so important for inmates to have the opportunity to work at a suitable prison job, to go to school and express themselves through art or music, because someday most of them will return to the free world.

The question is will society take them back into its ranks and accept the time they served as just punishment? Will these men be given the chance to better themselves after they've survived the agony of incarceration? Many people in the free world have a twisted and inaccurate view of prison life. Television news reports, along with crime dramas and other media, exaggerate the fact that inmates have cable TV, enjoy ice cream, and lift weights. What many outsiders fail to recognize is that the harshest punishment a man experiences during his incarceration is the total loss of his freedom. The constant reminder that he is not an individual, only a number, devastates a man's soul. Adding to this misery is that many of the prisoners' families forget about them, as do their friends, colleagues, and intimate partners. Worst off of all are the female inmates, for they experience abandonment more intensely than males. It is my opinion that being incarcerated is an even harsher crueler punishment for the human soul than for the body.

Our hope, as responsible and caring members of corrections, is that we can help them during their incarceration in order to prepare them for reentry into society as productive and creative citizens. Sadly, little if any, rehabilitation services exist for recidivists.

I'll always appreciate Alex, the Man of Stone, and the risk he took when he stood up and let me know I was not alone. His expression never changed in the many weeks I had the honor of having him in my class. I always felt like I was in the presence of someone who had a vision of something unknown. When I told Joe about my appreciation for the unexpected help from my stone-faced student, he simply smiled and said, "We try to take care of our teachers at the Ellis Unit."

Blood Path

Prison routine is sometimes interrupted by unexpected circumstances. Every morning at a quarter to six, the teachers walked down through the gym to the inmate-dining hall to fetch our students for the first day's class. On this particular day, I had just myself poured a hot cup of coffee. It was a little too hot, so I carried it gingerly as I chatted with the other teachers as we walked over to find our students. It was just another morning at Ellis.

Little did we know that during breakfast, an inmate had been shanked fourteen times. We had just turned the corner to enter the gym when we came upon two inmates who were carrying the dying man to the infirmary. Blood gushed from his numerous wounds, leaving a thick crimson stream that stretched the length of the gym and down the main hallway to the dining hall.

It all kind of happened in slow motion: one teacher fainted while the others choked back their breakfast and I spilled my coffee. I tried to salvage what I could but it didn't matter anymore. I didn't want to drink or smell anything after seeing such a sight so early in the morning.

We hurried over to the dining hall and took our time collecting the day's students, but there was no way to avoid the three-foot wide path of blood on the way back. The inmate had been killed in the only hallway that ran from the school area to the dining hall. Still, I wanted to get it over with, so I was the first to gather up my class and begin the march back.

A lone inmate had begun to mop up the blood, but to call it "mopping" would be a stretch. "Spreading thin" is more like it. There was just so much of it, but it didn't seem to bother him. It also didn't faze any of my students.

Wherever they go in a prison, inmates are required to walk along a single designated path from which they are *never* permitted to stray. This path usually runs along the wall of every hallway and corridor, and no inmate can step out of it at any time, for any reason. That rule applied to the two inmates who had carried away the body of the slain inmate. As a result, the designated walkway was covered in spilled blood for much of the way. Still, it seemed to make no difference to my students. They trawled through the puddles of blood with nary a word or look that anything was wrong, leaving a path of red footprints with their prison-made shoes. It was surreal that something so ghastly to us teachers could seem so insignificant to inmates.

When I got back to the classroom, I found Joe had already poured me a fresh cup of coffee.

"Mr. Humphries," he said somberly, "that man who died this morning was family to one of your students." He gestured over at an African American inmate who was sitting in the back of the class. "It was his first cousin."

"Thanks Joe. I'll give him our condolences during morning break."

Later during our smoke break, I walked up to the inmate whose cousin had died and said quietly, "I'm sorry to hear your cousin was killed this morning."

"It don't bother me," he answered shortly. "He should've changed the channel last night."

He lit a hand-rolled cigarette and just stared off into space. In this often, bizarre world of prison life, an argument over a TV show can easily become a life-or-death situation. It reminded me of how insignificant the murder of an inmate is in this world.

Between the shadow and the light lies the gray zone of apathy, where the beast lays waiting to ravage its next victim.

Satan's Disciple

One day, as Joe was helping the students get their supplies and projects out, I glanced out the windows facing the front of Ellis. The exterior window sill reeked from its deep layer of pigeon droppings, though a few feet in front of the window I could see the back of a cast stone screen that gave visitors the impression of a clean façade. I wondered how many pounds of pigeon poo lay between the window and that pristine screen. I'd been asking for years to have it cleaned up. "We'll look into it," was the usual administrative response, but that never happened. During my three years at Ellis, the black-and-white layers of pigeon poo only grew thicker.

The students settled down to their class work. Most of them were painting acrylic paintings on canvas board. The others drew pictures with soft pastels on colored pastel paper. With my morning coffee in my hand, faithfully prepared by Joe, I began strolling among my students, observing their progress and making little suggestions as I passed by.

Then, suddenly, a strange sensation came over me. It was a somewhat familiar feeling, but one I had only felt while visiting death row or the psychiatric treatment center. It was the same pulsating vibration I got when walking among the most wretched of the men in the treatment center. Gradually, my pulse grew stronger and I grew more uncomfortable. It's hard to put into words how awful these sensations felt. It made the coffee taste sour and the air cold and wet. And it seemed to be coming from out in the hallway.

I stepped into the doorway, keeping one eye on my class. With my other eye, I saw the feeble frame of a dark haired, Caucasian inmate coming down the hall toward the classroom. He humbly hobbled toward me on an aluminum crutch that had been fitted around his left arm. The moment we looked at each other, the vibrations stopped. I had never seen or heard of this man before, so what happened next was a surprise to the both of us.

"You are not to seek any new disciples here," I declared in a commanding voice, my words springing unbidden from the deepest part of my soul. *"You may work in my class like any other student but you will not be permitted to seek any converts here!"* I was as surprised at the words as was the crippled inmate. Even my voice didn't sound like my own.

The two of us stood for a moment, eyes fixed on one another. I felt transfixed by the presence of the purest evil. I noticed the inmate wore an upside down pentagram suspended from a thin silver chain hanging around his neck. Shifting his weight on his aluminum crutch, he said, "How did you know who I am?"

"I felt your presence as you approached my classroom." My own voice had returned.

His eyes narrowed, trying in earnest to pierce my aura and seize upon my heart and fill it with fear.

"Oh, I get it. You're one of those people who can sense our presence." He sneered at me as he hobbled towards the doorway of my classroom. Every bit of my soul told me that this man was evil, pure evil, but nevertheless, I let him enter my classroom.

Since I began working in the prison system, I had begun to develop a sort of "sixth sense" for certain psychic phenomena. My ability to sense these things was not voluntary or intentional. It just happened. When I had felt similar impressions or visions earlier in my life, I dismissed them as happenstance. But now, there was no mistaking it. Whatever was going on in me was real, and I had to learn how to live with it. Even though I had started acting upon these impressions, I kept the source of them a secret. I had a family now, and couldn't let my superiors think I was becoming unstable.

When the students, including the new one, left for their noon meal, Joe called me to one side with a worried look: "Mr. Humphries, that new student is very bad news!"

"I know."

"Did you know he's *the* High Priest of the satanic cult here?"

"Yeah, Joe, I kind of figured that one out too."

"You know what that means to all the guys locked up," he went on. "When someone has to get done, he's the man for that sort of thing. No one crosses him, not even the guards."

"Well, I guess even disciples of Satan have a right to an education in my class, but I did tell him he'd better keep doing only art and nothing else."

"You did what?" Joe's eyes widened at my response. "Bad news, Mr. Humphries, *baaad news!*"

Satan's priest remained in class for a week or two, then abruptly stopped attending. Several months later, one of the guards showed me a handwritten note that been intercepted.

"Someone wants to murder Joe, your assistant," the guard said. It was an order for murder and two names I recognized were on it. "Looks like the other inmate is one of your students. You wouldn't happen to know what this is about?"

"Well, the handwriting looks familiar." I answered. I had a hunch who was behind it.

"May I borrow this for a while?" I asked.

"I'm not supposed to let you do that," the guard answered bluntly.

"Okay. But what if I told you I have a pretty good idea as to who wrote this?"

"I can't release evidence on a hunch, Mr. Humphries." Then he looked down at his watch. "But I'll tell you what: You can take the note while I'm having lunch. One hour. That's all you got." Ten minutes was all I needed. I went to the files from the two-week period during which the satanic priest was in my class, and pulled his paper work. The handwriting was an exact match.

That afternoon the guard and I took the evidence to Mr. Tracy's replacement, Principal Landry who examined the note and the artwork. "You've done some pretty good detective work here, Mr. Humphries."

"Thank you, sir. But I couldn't have done it without the help of the guards."

"Is that right?" he asked, looking at the guard.

"Yes sir," answered the guard. "I noticed that both of the names on the kill order were in the art program, so I went straight to Mr. Humphries.

"Fine work, gentlemen." Principal Landry handed out praise only when he meant it. "Y'all may have averted a couple of homicides. I'll set up an appointment with the warden immediately."

Within the hour, the three of us were in Warden Savage's office. He sat for a moment, inspecting the kill order and the art notes.

"Well, the handwriting does match but he didn't sign it," said the warden.

"With all due respect, Warden Savage, we all know who wrote it," I answered back.

"No one here doubts that, Mr. Humphries, but we can't prove anything. So the best thing to do is transfer your assistant to another prison unit and then see what's best for your other student."

That other student was already scheduled for parole, but, sadly, he was also dying from terminal cancer. As result, Warden Savage moved the release date up so he could go home to Austin and spend his last days with his family.

Joe was transferred to the Ramsey II Unit a day later, a safer environment where he worked as an education department assistant. I missed him greatly and never did find a suitable replacement. He was honest and hardworking, an uncommon quality in a world of con men and twisted morals. As for Satan's Disciple, I never saw him again.

Mr. Gordon

Mr. Gordon taught math at the Ellis Unit. His imposing six-foot plus height and burly African American frame commanded respect from his students, yet he always exuded patience and compassion. We carpooled together for years, and even though I got to know him as well as anyone did, he kept some things to himself.

Then, during Christmas time one year, our relationship started to change. All the teachers had mixed feelings about leaving for the holidays, because we knew how hard it would be for our students to spend this time of the year alone. Still, it didn't kill our holiday spirit. There was the usual press of loved ones from out of town and helping of our children mail their wish lists to Santa Claus. My church choir, needing my baritone voice for their Yuletide caroling, competed with the party invitations received from colleagues wanting to show off a new home. It was wonderful time to spend with family and friends.

We said our goodbyes to the prison inmate staff and wished each other a Merry Christmas. The holiday season is hardest on the inmates and saddest time of year for them. We all knew some of them would attempt suicide, contemplate escape, or murder another inmate while we were enjoying our holiday dinners. Tempers would flare in the stark loneliness of prison isolation, calling forth the worst a man could do to another. That was a time where the beast roams free within prison walls to further prey on the hearts of the men trapped inside the steel and concrete confines of a maximum-security prison. Prison guards were not immune to this either. Spending Christmas Day on-duty inside prison walls instead of spending it with their families is a hard burden. And so, in our hearts, we prayed that God would watch over the security personnel and our students during those long, lonely days ahead.

As for Mr. Gordon, I returned from the holidays to find him seeming a little off. As I climbed into the passenger seat of his pale yellow Chrysler, I asked, "How was your Christmas?"

He glanced at me from the corner of his eye, as though considering his reply.

"Okay. Everything went as we expected."

This was an odd response. So was the drive to work that day. We may have said less than five words to each other as we drove to Ellis. Something, was bothering him, I just knew it. Eventually, he told me that his Christmas hadn't been an easy one. His brother had finally lost his battle against cancer and passed away over the holiday break.

It must have been hard on Mr. Gordon, because he never returned to his old self after that. Every time I saw him, he was lost in thought: physically there but mentally somewhere else. I noticed a faraway look in his eyes. I had seen that look before, in James, the Native American, and Alex, the Man of Stone. Mr. Gordon seemed to be gazing at something the rest of us could not see. Whatever vision possessed these men, it seemed to bring them a soulful peace. But even though he was a different man now, Mr. Gordon never missed a day of work and continued to do an excellent job.

Then, one morning as he arrived to pick me up, he appeared especially cheerful, like his old self. He wished me good morning and I returned the greeting and asked how he was.

"Good. Real good." He paused for a few moments, grinning slightly. "I just bought a home, Jim. Going to set it up on my family's land."

"Well, congratulations! I had no idea! Where are you moving to?"

That was when he revealed one of his secrets. Before working for Windham, he had been teaching for Job Corps in New Braunsfels, when finally he decided to take possession of property deeded to his family after the Civil War as freed slaves! He told me the details one afternoon as we drove over to see his new home and land, located in an area south of Huntsville known to locals as "Freedman's Land." Many former slaves' families were given land in this area by the State of Texas after they were emancipated.

Mr. Gordon spoke with a mixture of pain and pride as

he told the story of his family. He was proud of his roots, knowing everything a man should know about his ancestors and history. That day I met his mother, his wife and her mother. The Gordons gave me a warm welcome, almost as if they had been expecting my visit for some time. Though it was the first time I had ever met any of them, we talked like old friends rather than mere acquaintances.

That's also when I realized his entire family shared the same expression of serene confidence. They made you feel like there was nothing to worry about, that the world was unfolding as it should. It felt like being a kid again, when we were free to just enjoy the day and not worry about tomorrow. They never made me feel like I owed them anything just because I was white and a Southerner.

There were deep divisions in the Huntsville community between the races at this time, but, still, a mutual respect for each other's rights and culture always remained. No one can change the past and what our forefathers endured. The only things we can do are to make the best of the present and ensure positive changes for the future.

That fall Mr. Gordon stopped eating the delicious, home-cooked meals his wife packed for him daily. Then he stopped eating lunch altogether. Through all that, he never complained about his health. He continued to teach, working every day without as much as slowing his stride. Our carpool rides were filled with talk about home projects he was working on. He was very proud of his new home, but it became clear to me that he was sick.

When I first met Mr. Gordon, he weighed a hard, two hundred twenty pounds. Always a good looking man, he cared about his appearance, but over time his face started to look drawn and old beyond his years. Another Christmas came and went, and still he kept quiet about his health. A few weeks after the New Year, he checked in to Huntsville Memorial Hospital for pancreatic cancer treatment. Principal Landry called the faculty together one afternoon to announce the reason for Mr. Gordon's absence, and that he was going to approve him for medical retirement. It was a sad day for everyone.

Three days before his death, I went to his home for one last visit. He looked like he weighed no more than a hundred twenty pounds, but that hadn't slow him down. I found him lying in a yellow chaise lounge in his front yard, barking out orders at his nephews as they tore at the thick brush. He looked up at me, smiled broadly, and asked me what I thought he should do with the landscaping. It broke my heart to see him so gaunt and frail, but he couldn't have seemed happier, sitting aloft a yellow throne, surveying his land.

His funeral was held at a small Baptist church near his home. His family asked me to say a few words on his behalf. I rose from my seat and stood in front of the small African American congregation. A surge of strength and thankfulness filled my whole body. I felt very honored to share this moment with them.

"Mr. Gordon was my colleague, but he was also my friend. We carpooled together for the past several years and we laughed about the crazy things our students at Ellis would do. But during a time of great personal suffering and pain, he never complained or gave anyone at work any indication of his personal problems. He was a gentleman in every manner of speaking. He could be both stern and compassionate, and never once did he miss day of work. He was a man anyone could depend on."

"Amen," answered the congregation.

"He never lost his professional focus, even when his body was ailing him. He lived up to his duty to teach math students at the Ellis State Prison Farm until the very end," I continued.

"Amen!"

I looked around at his family and friends, all gathered to celebrate the passing of this good man. Not a single tear could be seen falling from their faces. Instead, each person expressed a stoic pride in Mr.

Gordon's accomplishments. Memories of the good times we shared flooded my head, of how proud he was to have his plot of land. I don't remember if it was from the sorrow at his loss or pride at having known him, but I felt as if my heart would burst.

"Mr. Gordon's life has taught me two invaluable lessons," I said, my voice cracking. "That life's too short to spend it complaining about small things. And that it is never too late . . . to come home."

He was buried among his family in an old freedman's cemetery. At last, Mr. Gordon had truly come home. May he rest in peace under the tall East Texas pines of Freedman's Land.

Parting of the Ways

Art Supervisor

"MR. HUMPHRIES, GLAD YOU WERE able to make it on such a short notice." Her years of working seemed to have little effect on Dr. Murray. She looked as vibrant as she had when we first met in 1972, nearly thirteen years before.

"I'd like to promote you to the position of art supervisor for Windham," she continued. "You're going to develop, improve and coordinate art programs with the other art teachers. We'll need you to help design art classrooms on prison farms, manage all of the inmate art shows, and formulate a functional curriculum guide. But this job will require constant travel and more hours of commitment that you've probably ever experienced. So before you give me an answer, I'd like you think this through thoroughly and call me with your decision."

That night I discussed it with my wife, and we both agreed it would be a good move for my career.

At first, I enjoyed the challenge. I enjoyed working with other art teachers and the responsibility of managing the prison art shows. But the long trips across endless miles of Texas highways to distant prison farms began to take its toll. Since prisons never increase the

175

property values of their surrounding areas, they are typically located in remote, unheard-of locations. As a result most of my time was spent on the road.

The bigger paycheck and more freedom to plan my work schedule were a great help for a while, but they both came at a steep price. On nearly every trip, other supervisors would cram into the same, stifling TDC-issued car with me, where the air conditioning rarely, if ever, worked. Our budget only allowed for rooms at second-rate motels, usually a smoker's room. No matter how much I scrubbed and bathed myself in Old Spice aftershave, I couldn't get rid of that ashtray odor.

But none of those things affected me as much as the extra time I had to spend away from my family. Compared to staying at home where I could play with my children and paint in my own art studio, sleeping in a smoke-stained motel room was no pleasure at all.

Not to mention the kind of food I sometimes found myself eating.

Court-Ordered Food

While I was working with Windham, a federal court issued an order that required the food that prisons served to their officers and employees should be of the same quality that they served to the inmates. Naturally, most prison units responded by improving the quality of all of their food. However, at least one prison did not, as I found out when I had the pleasure of visiting the Darrington Unit, where they had their own unique interpretation of said precedent. The one and only time I ever ate there was more than fifteen years ago, yet I still cringe when I recall what they served for dinner that day.

Any prison dining experience can be gauged properly by simply watching the expressions on the faces of employees when they look at the menu. It's also helpful to take notice of how the staff and officers eat: Do they even look at what they're eating? Or do they cover it all with globs of condiments? Sometimes their facial expressions alone are enough to kill the most ravenous appetite.

That day, as I approached the serving line at Darrington, nothing on the serving tables looked remotely appetizing to me. The meat sauce mixture was beyond the definition of mystery meat. Pools of fat floated above a sub-layer of a non-homogeneous substance. A nearby pan of sticky, white mush turned out to be rice. Another massive pan that smelled like lawn clippings followed, but upon closer inspection appeared to be collard greens. And that was it. I had forgone chowing down on a steak with the other supervisors for a meal of sludge, mush and lawn clippings.

I'd left my meal ticket at the bottom of a locked drop box, so it was too late to back out now. I was about to lose all hope when, by the grace of God, I spotted a mound of generic white bread. I took my plate, piled on several slices of bread and prayed the coffee had not been brewed from charcoal.

I took a seat that gave me a clear view of the Darrington chow line, so I could keep an eye on how their officers and staff reacted. An older officer charged in and immediately loaded his plate with slop. He sat down and shoveled down huge mouthfuls, never looking at what he was eating. The other officers who sat with him ate about the same portions in the same hurried manner, feverishly gulping down forkfuls of lawn clippings and mush to shorten the time they had to endure the taste.

Then a group of very large, athletic officers in black uniforms with metal pipes hanging from their belts swarmed in. Someone had told me earlier that these officers were the S.W.A.T. squad assigned to Darrington in an effort to quell recent violence. Their approach was, to say the least, comical. Their booming laughter and loud conversations immediately ceased when they reached the serving line. A dead silence fell as each officer stood holding his plate, unhappy with his grim culinary choice.

Some took the mush. Others were bolder and lumped a side of lawn clippings beside their mush. Not a single one of them braved the vat of sludge. A few of them came to the same conclusion I did: They piled on a loaf's worth of bread on their barren plates. One even had the gall to ask the inmate kitchen workers if there was anything else to eat, but they ignored the guards anyway, staring off into space with a look of total disinterest. I'd seen enough for one evening. And the bread I choked down was actually stale, and yes, the coffee had been brewed from charcoal.

The End of the Trail

The part of my job I loved most was promoting the Traveling Prison Art Shows. The success of three spectacular art shows, held in Waco, College Station and Houston, started what I presumed would be just the beginning of many years of art shows. Collectors from across the Southwest flocked to the Texas Prison Rodeo every year, all vying for a piece of authentic prison artwork. Occasionally I got the feeling that some of them were in it for only for the sensationalism, not the quality of the art; that they wanted an example of rough prison life that they could show off while gossiping about the artist's horrible crimes. Collectors would brag to me about how much they could sell a portrait or landscape for, then turn right around and complain that the $10 price tag was too expensive.

My 1985 show had just been booked at Zilker Park in Austin when I was informed the plug was being pulled on the Traveling Art Show. Then in February 1985, I was reassigned to the position of a general supervisor. Soon, all of the subject area supervisors, from art to math to music, became generic supervisors. They kept me at a supervisor's pay grade, but they made it clear my job had nothing to do with art.

On October 26, 1986, the Texas Prison Rodeo shut its doors forever, effectively killing the Rodeo Art Show as well. Then the very successful Traveling Art Show was eliminated. For a brief period, Windham hosted an Inmate Art Show in their administration building on the Wynne Unit property, but even that didn't last long. With the passage of H.R. 5484 of 1986, the U.S. Congress and President Ronald Reagan's administration made it clear what direction the American penal system would go in.

H.R. 5484 changed everything, even before it was enacted into law. Gone were the days of rehabilitative care. Now a new era of increased sentences was upon us, one that would strain the capacity of every prison in America, prisons that would soon become overcrowded. Monies that were originally earmarked for enrichment classes like mine, were diverted into building more space to house the growing prison population and hiring more security personnel. The top priority now was punishment. There would be no room for enrichment.

Life at Windham wasn't the same after that. I spent week after week on the road, giving standardized tests to Windham teachers. Sometimes I walked by classrooms full of dusty school furniture, rooms once full of men who could discover more about themselves through two hours of painting than they would by sitting in their cells for years on end.

Outside my classroom, they were inmates scorned by society, forgotten by their families. But once inside my art class, they became free men. Their imaginations flourished and memories came to life. Their pains and frustrations could be openly expressed with canvas and color. During all the years I taught these men, I heard them say the same words over and over again:

"This art class is the best part of my week."

"My life has a new meaning now because I'm good at something."

"No one ever believed I was any good, but you do."

Now it seemed like the art programs were being stymied completely. And that was just the start. I could read the proverbial handwriting on the wall. And I didn't like it.

One morning, I hurried over to Dr. Lane Murray's office, still smelling of cheap motel soap from another night out on the road. She kindly let me express my concerns before she told me about the changes that were coming. The political winds had shifted. Voters and legislators were demanding stricter guidelines with more rigid sentences. Taxpayers didn't want to see their tax dollars go to art classes for inmates. After the shift from a rehabilitative to a more punitive parole system, along with new minimum sentencing guidelines for drug-related offenses, prison populations began to increase nationwide. Funds were rerouted from all programs considered nonessential and funneled into plans to build more prisons to house all the new convicts.

The Windham School System was a different place in 1985; much different from the one I had joined in 1972. I had given so much to this, and blazed a trail for a program I believed would be integral to a prisoner's experience.

I resigned again, this time for good. Within a few years of my resignation, every single inmate art program was eliminated.

Before my last day, Dr. Murray paid me a visit.

"I want you to know I appreciate all work you've done here," she said. "These years have been good to us. I am just so sorry to see you go."

"Thank you, Dr. Murray. But this place has changed." I was watching a line of sullen inmates marching back to their cells. "The inmates are the same but Windham has changed. I don't belong here anymore."

"I understand," she answered, paused, and then started again. "You know, you're really passionate about art. We all saw it in your work. And I've never known anyone as talented as you. It's like we had our own Rembrandt walking around."

"Yeah, I hear that's what they call me."

"It's true. You have a gift, Mr. Humphries, not only for portraits and painting, but for understanding people. You've helped so many of our students do something they could be proud of. They will miss you. Everyone at Windham will miss you, including me."

Her words made me feel better, considering the current state of affairs at Windham. Only the most basic education was now required of every unit, and when I write basic I mean, "free from enrichment courses." Politicians consider art to be of little or no value in the sphere of adult basic education. Granted, a correctional institution can measure and improve a man's academic skills, but in my opinion, it cannot effectively care for a man's soul. Only the inmate's religious practice was lawfully protected, so only that was offered. Art was axed.

EPILOGUE

THE BORN-AGAIN CHRISTIAN facing a date with the executioner gets more media coverage than a convicted murderer who will show and sell paintings he had produced legally while doing his time. Today in Texas, at the turn of the millenium, inmate artists may create art or approved crafts by special permission, in the piddling shop or with a piddling card in his cell. But the word piddling is defined as "an action spent aimlessly doing something insignificant, trifling, or petty." The expression of the human spirit is none of these!

The word "penitentiary" originated from the Latin *paenitentia*, meaning "repentance." I now understand that a prison sentence is not merely a time spent, cut off from the free world, but it can also be a time for reflection and rehabilitation. I believe that every human needs an outlet to re-create their life, reflect on the choices they have made, and express the unquantifiable needs of the human spirit. I am happy to have given almost thirteen years in pursuit of this belief, and to be able to write these words, so you too can learn from, ponder on, and even laugh, at these stories.

The incredible pain and suffering I witnessed during my years at Windham led me to several conclusions. In a moment of confusion and extreme emotion–such as envy, fear or anger—the beast will momentarily open the door to seemingly attractive or unavoidable alternatives to acceptable human behavior. This beast lives within us all, and it can never be defeated. The beast is as much a part of you and me as it is of these inmates whose stories I've shared with you.

You must take daily care of the beast within by listening to what it wants and when it starts to scratch at your conscience. The beast feeds on your fears and insecurities, so when it begins to claw away, take heed by looking carefully at your life. Find the source of the beast's strength and face this with courage. Selfish darkness must be tempered by compassionate light. By knowing you too can succumb to the will of the beast, that you are just as human and vulnerable to making the same terrible mistakes as these inmates, you will have already made yourself stronger.

Too often I heard an inmate cry foul and say they didn't do it because they were high on drugs and alcohol, and surely would have never dreamed of committing their crime, if only they were sober. Irresponsible use of alcohol is a prime path into the world of the mirror image value system I witnessed at Huntsville. Once a man finds himself on the other side of society's moral looking glass, he may find it easier to be drawn deep into the irrational world of drug abuse, selfish excess, destructive hysteria, and mindless aggression. I find it hard to understand how grown men can come up with every excuse under the sun to justify their crime, while ignoring the fact that they chose to act lawlessly.

Regardless, the many years of working for Windham, alongside dedicated teachers and administrators, and working with the brave men and women in security and treatment, at so many different places in Texas, has taught me that there are people who have a great capacity to care for a forsaken man.

Yet, despite the convicts' capacity for self-delusion regarding their crimes, they are still human, still deserving of humane treatment, and they still deserve a chance to express themselves through art.

— James L. Humphries

About the Authors

SOLDIER, ARTIST AND TEACHER: This is the order in which Jim Humphries' three concurrent careers entered his life.

Born November 27, 1935, in Louisville, Kentucky, James Lane Humphries was raised in Jackson, Mississippi. After graduating from Central High School in 1954, he went on active duty with the U.S. Marine Corps. In 1995, he retired as a U.S. Army Master Sergeant, after 28 years of combined military service with the Marine Corps, Texas Army National Guard, and the U.S. Army Reserve.

While in college, he began a career as an illustrator and artist. In 1961 he graduated from Millsaps College with a B.A. degree in mathematics. For ten years he worked as a technical illustrator, designer and artist, primarily for aerospace companies, before he began teaching in Texas public schools in 1968. In 1971 he earned a master's degree in education, with an emphasis on art, from Sam Houston State University in Huntsville, Texas. James spent the rest of his life teaching visual art to student of all ages, both young and old, free and incarcerated.

He was still teaching when he was diagnosed with brain cancer in December 2000. The world lost a wonderful man eight months later. His wife Celeste, his four children and five grandchildren survive him.

Jonathan R. Humphries is Jim's second son with Celeste. He currently resides in California, where he continues to write and teach music. This is his first published work.

ACKNOWLEDGMENTS

THIS BOOK WOULD NOT HAVE BEEN possible without the support and generosity of Rev. Robert Lukosh & Mrs. Leslee Lukosh, Yin Ling Leung, Landon Steele, Xiaolei Kerr, Chris Mesel, and Adrienne Howell.

A special thank you to Nathan and Marion Haase, of Haase Photography, for the amazing photos; Jim Willett of the Texas Prison Musuem, for allowing us access to the mural paintings; Thomas Burchfield and Jim Aikin, for your excellent line editing; Henner Zeller, for your technical expertise; Charity VanDeberg, for your friendship and writer's touch; Elsa Marie Suberbielle, for believing in me when I did not and for keeping me focused when I wanted to give up; and my mother, Elizabeth Coiman-Lopez, for providing the back story to so many untold tales, and for making my father the happiest man alive. I love you, Mom.

ART CREDITS

Cover art—inmate portait by Jim Humphries

Portaits and sketches by Jim Humphries: pg. 16, 26, 37, 54, 69, 74, 80, 85, 87, 138, 147, 155, 160, 164, 171

Photos of inmate mural paintings, courtesy of Texas Prison Museum & Nathan Haase Photography: pg. 65, 94, 95, 98, 105, 109

Original oil painting by Joe Mason, gifted to Jim Humphries: pg. 150

Made in the USA
Lexington, KY
16 September 2013